NEW ENGLAND
IN A NUTSHELL

Steve Jermanok

Published 2020
Printed in the United States of America
Print ISBN: 978-1735173702
Ebook ISBN: 978-1735173719

Active Travels
89 Roundwood Rd
Newton MA 02464
https://activetravels.com

Table of Contents

Introduction

In 1996, a week before the birth of our child, Jake, I received a copy of the first book I authored, *Outside Magazine's Adventure Guide to New England.* I had spent the entirety of the prior year traversing the region in every season as I sampled the many trails, bike paths, rivers, lakes, and Atlantic Ocean as much as humanly possible, hiking two mountains a day if I could. Honestly, I couldn't get enough of the outdoors, gleefully paddling down remote rivers or mountain biking deep in the woods and laughing out loud that I'm getting paid to do this! Little did I realize, it would lead to a very rewarding career as a freelance travel writer, writing more than 2,000 articles, and working on another 8 books. I would travel the globe, but just as often, return to discover another gem in my backyard, New England. To celebrate the 25th anniversary of my first book, I did a deep dive into the hundreds of stories I've written on the region for the *Boston Globe, Yankee Magazine, Boston Magazine, Boston Herald,* and many other publications. I distilled those stories down to their essence, eliminating fat, while updating and revising the copy. The result is what I believe is a definitive guide to the region, *New England in a Nutshell.*

Instead of authoring a typical guidebook, where far too many pages are devoted to topics I care very little about like topography, I resorted to my favorite form of journalism, the round-up article. Perhaps it's my background as a chemical engineer, but I appreciate lean, succinct writing, especially when it comes to something as pragmatic as a guidebook. I want to get to the point quickly and tell you my favorite fall foliage routes, lobster shacks, art historical finds, and more than 50 other topics in this book. There's no better way to deliver this material than in short form so you can quickly peruse the subject and get there as soon as possible. Rest assured that these are my favorite picks, the one percent that made the cut. For example, I have visited over 1,000 inns this past quarter century in New England and I've only included my top 12 in that chapter.

It's amazing how easily the outdoors section of this book stood the test of time, having to do very little updating or revising. In fact, I have no doubt that the exceptional ridge walk between Mount Lincoln and Mount Lafayette in the White Mountains will be the top hike to take a century from now. If no one else reads this book, I can take pride knowing that I've given my grandchildren a guide to the finest locales in New England. Most resorts and inns have also stood the test of time. Restaurants are the lone category that didn't fare as well. Those James Beard winners of the past like L'Espalier and Hamersley's Bistro in Boston are unfortunately no longer with us. So instead of including high-end dining, I chose to put the spotlight on clam shacks like Woodman's, which has been around since 1914, and pizza joints like Frank Pepe Pizzeria Napoletana, in operation in New Haven since 1925.

I'm grateful to be joined by my wife, Lisa Leavitt, whose photos have graced many of my stories for the *Boston Globe*. Most importantly, I'm grateful to all those editors who gave me the opportunity to write, including Arthur Frommer who delivered that first book deal to me so many years ago. I'm also blessed that you had the interest to pick up this book, or at least, download it to your phone. Thank you for your continued support!

Steve Jermanok
Newton, Massachusetts
June 11, 2020

For the Romantic

3 Requisite Fall Foliage Drives

The beginning of autumn in America is a time to savor the last precious moments of summer against the countryside's mosaic of reds, yellows, oranges, purples, and golds, before the chill of winter enters the air and the trees grow barren. This is not news to most of us. Indeed, leaf peeping has become cliché. There are 24-hour toll-free hotlines in most states to keep you informed of nature's progress, even web cams pointed at maples to show you the daily change. And then there's the traffic. It seems like the entire population of New York City and Boston is behind the wheels of a car on congested New England roadways.

Thus, the reason I've tried to avoid the mainstream routes so you can truly appreciate the kaleidoscopic splendor. After all, a fall foliage road trip is more than a mere drive. It also incorporates apple picking, tasting cider and hot doughnuts, and perhaps most importantly leaving your vehicle behind to take a much-needed scenic walk to a lonely waterfall, where autumn's colors reflect off the water. Here are my top three picks:

Route 100, Vermont

Don't believe the Vermont fall foliage hype? All it takes is one drive on Route 100 from Stowe to Weston to understand the allure. Traveling along the ridgeline of the 4,000-foot Green Mountains, whose carpeted slopes radiate with the multi-hued maples, you can't help but sing its praises. First stop is Stowe. Unlike many New England ski areas, where all amenities are found on a road leading to the mountain resulting in the look of a strip mall, Stowe grew up around a centuries old Vermont village. The charm of skiing Stowe is that you can leave the mountain behind and stroll down Main Street (Route 100) past the requisite white steeple atop Stowe Community Church. Go inside **Shaw's General Store**, open since 1895, to purchase a flannel shirt and you've been transported back in time.

Heading south on Route 100, you'll want to visit the **Cold Hollow Cider Mill** for your jug of cider, out-of-the-oven doughnuts, and genuine maple syrup. Nearby is the **Ben and Jerry's factory**, where you can take a tour, sample the wares, and find out how the duo started their celebrated business. If you're hungry, get slightly off Route 100 in the town of Warren. With its covered bridge, post office, town hall, church, and country store, all on Main Street, this is rural America at its most genuine. Stop at the **Warren Country Store**, where you can grab one of their large sandwiches to eat on picnic tables next to the Mad River.

Soon you'll be driving through the farming community of Rochester to take that requisite "cows and meadow" shot. In Weston, you can find all your Vermont souvenirs at the **Vermont Country Store**. This is no mom-and-pop country store, but a large purveyor of Vermont goods that first opened in 1946. That includes syrup, a vast selection of Vermont cheeses, a mouth-watering candy selection (including the addictive lemon drops), bird feeders, polar fleece jackets, and impractical fare like Tired Old Ass bath salts and Slinkies.

Kancamagus Highway, New Hampshire

The problem with the yearly fall foliage driving trip is that one person has to drive. Your companion revels in the bright colors, spewing expletives of joy, while you barely catch a glimpse of the scenery. That's why we relish routes like the 34-mile Kancamagus Highway (Route 112) or "Kanc" as the locals call it, where you can stop at numerous trailheads, slow down, and walk through the foliage. At 3,000 feet, the Kanc snakes through the verdant forests and granite cliffs of the White Mountains. To immerse yourself in the scenery, try the Boulder Loop Trail, which begins at the Covered Bridge Campground, 6 miles west of Conway. The 2.8-mile circuit takes about three hours to complete and provides vistas of Mount Chocorua. Or perhaps you want to bag Chocorua itself. The trailhead for the climb is on the Kanc, 11.5 miles from Route 16 in Conway. The hike is 7.6 miles round-trip and takes 6 to 7 hours. If the climb up Chocorua is too strenuous, at least visit Champney Falls on the same trail for views of a pristine waterfalls.

The Mohawk Trail, Massachusetts

High above the Berkshire Hills in western Massachusetts, the Mohawk Trail (Route 2) has been a local favorite for touring since the road was built in 1914. Drive the most scenic stretch of road from Shelburne Falls to the home of Williams College, Williamstown. In Charlemont, the rapids of the Deerfield River come into view. Then you rise high above the Deerfield Valley, with views of farmland and forest below. There are a handful of hokey souvenir shops along the road that have been around since the 50s. Soon, you'll make a hairpin turn into the industrial town of North Adams, where you'll find **Mass MoCA**, one of the largest centers for contemporary art in the United States. Continue on Route 2 to the college town of Williamstown, home to the **Clark Art Institute**. Wander into their galleries to view an impressive collection of Impressionism, with canvases by Monet, Manet, Degas, Renoir, Cezanne, and an entire room devoted to American master Winslow Homer.

8 Summer Drives That Will Keep You Smiling

One doesn't drive in New England simply to get from Point A to Point B. No, we like to linger, savor the beauty, cherish the history. We're fortunate to be blessed with a diverse landscape full of majestic sights like the jagged shoreline of Maine, the granite notches of New Hampshire, the bucolic farmland of Vermont, and the long stretch of white beach found in Rhode Island. We stop not only to post photos to our Instagram and Facebook accounts, but to dine on lobster rolls and fried clams at renowned seafood shacks, hike on the same shoreline and forest paths that inspired Winslow Homer and Robert Frost, and stop to stay at legendary inns or a new cabin built into the vast Maine wilderness. These 8 drives will not disappoint:

A Painterly Perspective, Kennebunkport to Cape Elizabeth, Maine

Stick to the slower routes that hug the southern Maine shoreline (Routes 9 and 77) and you'll be treated to the same rugged landscape that inspired Winslow Homer to set up shop in Prouts Neck. Indeed, **Homer's Studio**, now open to the public thanks to a $10 million renovation done by the Portland Museum of Art, is one of the many highlights of this drive. Drop your bags off at the venerable **White Barn Inn** in Kennebunkport, which recently went through its own refurbishment, updating all 11 rooms and adding an outdoor sitting area. Then make your way past the 7-mile long Old Orchard Beach to Prouts Neck, where Homer would depict this craggy shoreline in its entirely from 1883 to 1910. Prearrange a tour of his simple 2-story studio with PMA and take the mile-long Cliff Walk atop the boulder-strewn shoreline to see the waves thrust up against the rock painted so brilliantly on his many canvases.

Onward to Cape Elizabeth on backcountry roads where glimpses of the ocean are always by your side. If you're feeling hungry, head to the beloved lobster-in-the-rough joint, **The Lobster Shack**. Order your food at the window of the rustic shack, wait for your number to be called, and grab a picnic table that rewards you with vistas of the Atlantic as it pours into Casco Bay framed by two lighthouses. Just down the road is arguably the most photographed and painted lighthouse on the New England coast and the last stop on this drive, the **Portland Head Light**. Built in 1791 and sitting on a bluff perched above the sea, the exquisite white edifice of the Portland Head Light has inspired the likes of Edward Hopper. Stroll around its 80-foot height and then hit the trails that line the shoreline. Lobstermen haul up traps from the back of their boats, while farther out to sea, oil tankers make their way in and out of Portland Harbor. Breathe in as much salty air as you need before making the return trip.

Connecticut River Amble, Old Saybrook to Hadlyme, Connecticut

Old Saybrook is where the Connecticut River meets the Long Island Sound, a good starting point for a drive that hugs the Connecticut River on Route 154. Start this drive south of Old Saybrook at Knollwood Beach on the Sound. Then continue north through cattails and salt marsh to the historic hub of Essex. In the mid-1800s, this section of the Connecticut River was lined with more than 50 shipyards. Boats would return from international waters with spices from the West Indies and ivory tusks from Zanzibar. The result of that newly acquired wealth are the large Colonial and Federal-style homes that border the water's edge and can be viewed as you continue north on Route 154.

In Tylerville, veer right on Route 82 across a drawbridge into East Haddam, site of the four-story gingerbread **Goodspeed Opera House**. Opened in 1877, this theater has staged the original productions of Annie and Shenandoah and still delivers three musicals a year. The Goodspeed is the mere opening number to the theatrics you'll soon see at your next stop, **Gillette Castle**. William Gillette amassed a fortune playing Sherlock Holmes on stage at the turn of last century, but judging from the Medieval-style fortress he designed on a vista overlooking the river, he would have been better suited to play King Arthur. You can tour the 24-room behemoth and walk the grounds over trestles and through tunnels, before heading downhill to the Hadlyme docks.

A Carpet of Velvety Green, St. Johnsbury to Lake Willoughby, Vermont

In a state known for its rural setting (only Wyoming and Alaska contain fewer people), the Northeast Kingdom is Vermont putting on its finest pastoral dress. Wave after wave of unspoiled hillside form a vast sea of green and small villages and farms spread out in the distance under a few soaring summits. Start this drive at the **St. Johnsbury Athenaeum**, where leather-bound books share space with a 19th-century art gallery, including Albert Bierstadt's monumental work, the 10-foot-by-15-foot Domes of the Yosemite. Across the street, the **Fairbanks Museum** is home to more than 3,000 preserved animals in glass cases, including a 1200-pound moose, an American Bison from 1902, and a Bengal Tiger.

Not surprising, this sylvan countryside is the perfect playground for outdoor activity. Continue north on Routes 5 and 114 to reach East Burke and the vast network of mountain bike trails called the **Kingdom Trails**. Riding on this soft forest passageway dusted with pine needles, and through century-old farms, the town has arguably created the finest off-road riding in New England. The huge barns that once housed the Jersey cows and Morgan horses of Elmer Darling in East Burke are now part of the 14-room **Inn at Mountain View Farm**, the obvious choice for spending the night and taking in this rural splendor. Continue north on Route 5A to one of the most stunning vistas in Vermont. Arriving at Lake Willoughby from the south, the dark blue waters come into view, dwarfed by faces of rock that stand directly across from each other—Mount Hor and Mount Pisgah. Cliffs plummet over 1,000 feet to the glacial waters below, in essence, creating a land-locked fjord. The scenery is best appreciated on the three-hour hike to the 2,751-foot summit of Mt. Pisgah. Afterwards, reward yourself with a dip in the cool waters of the lake.

Drive Through the Notches, Jackson to Dixville Notch, New Hampshire

The glacier that retreated 10,000-plus years ago to form the White Mountains seemed to have left in a hurry, without first smoothing the edges of the rocky detritus that remained. Narrow and steep mountainous passes, called notches, sharply cut through walls of granite that refused to budge. Driving through Crawford Notch, a sinuous 6-mile mountainous pass, has been a highly popular route since the stagecoach days.

Start this drive in the charming hamlet of Jackson and follow Route 302 West into the Notch. To truly appreciate this sculpture of granite, park your car at the Crawford Notch Visitor Center, former site of the Crawford railroad station, and take the hike up Mount Willard. In less than an hour, you'll make it to the peak where jaw-dropping views of Crawford Notch stand below you, a reward for your slight efforts. As soon as you leave Crawford Notch and continue on Route 302, the largest peak in New England, Mount Washington looms mightily above (or could very well be socked into the clouds). Situated in front of Mount Washington, like a sprawling wedding cake with scarlet frosting, is one of the grand dames of New England lodging, the **Mount Washington Hotel**. First opened in 1902, this National Historic Landmark has hosted such luminaries as Thomas Edison, Winston Churchill, and Alfred Hitchcock. You might want to drop your luggage off here and return that evening to dine downstairs at the American bistro, Stickney's. You can also choose to take the nearby **Cog Railway** and watch the coal-fired engines of this train dramatically climb the precipitous granite flanks that form Mount Washington.

To add another 3-hour loop to this drive, head north on Route 3 to Colebrook and follow Route 26 East to Dixville Notch, the narrowest notch in New Hampshire. Carved between Sanguinary Mountain and Mount Gloriette, the rocky cleft barely allows the two-lane road to squeeze through. Standing across from the once famous and now defunct Balsams Resort, the notch is now part of a state park, replete with waterfalls, flume and hiking trails. The short steep climb up to Table Rock leads to an exposed ledge that juts out over a cliff offering stupendous views.

Rhode Island Beach Ramble, Wickford to Watch Hill, Rhode Island

Far away from the crowds in Newport, the western half of Rhode Island's Narragansett Bay, is perfectly suited for a relaxed drive along the sea and marsh leading to small villages that have been summer getaways for over a century. Start in Wickford to watch the fishermen and sea kayakers navigate past the docked yachts in the quiet harbor. Follow

Route 1A South to reach the surfing community of Narragansett. In summer, the waves are much milder, attracting families who can easily walk to the lodging and restaurants in town. A wise choice is the boutique property, **The Break**, and their restaurant, Chair 5, featuring fresh oysters, lobster, and calamari straight off the docks.

Stop at the rock jetty at Roger Wheeler Memorial State Park in Galilee to watch the ferries come to and from Block Island. Then continue west past a series of popular beaches like East Matunuck State Beach in South Kingstown, petite-sized Blue Shutters Town Beach in Charlestown, and Misquamicut State Beach, Rhode Island's best honky-tonk beach. Atlantic Avenue's hotels, bars, restaurants, water slides, and miniature golf courses back seven miles of oceanfront. Ten minutes later, the Victorian-era homes clinging to the hillside are a sign that you arrived in the classic summer retreat of Watch Hill. Take a ride on one of the oldest carousels in the country, visit the small array of shops and restaurants, or opt for one of the finest coastal walks in the region at Napatree Point. Waves crash on your bare feet as you stroll on Napatree's crescent-shaped beach.

Cape Ann Cruise, Rockport to Ipswich, Massachusetts

Cape Ann is the other Cape, the one us New Englanders like to keep a coveted secret. Like Cape Cod, the miles of sublime beachfront are the region's number one attraction. But dig a little deeper and you'll find centuries-old New England villages to roam, the finest fried and steamed clams in the region, and wonderful opportunities to sea kayak in sheltered waters and to stroll along the Atlantic waters. Start in Rockport to walk the strip of shops known as Bearskin Neck. Art galleries share the street with restaurants on the piers that overlook Rockport's postcard-perfect harbor. A ten-minute drive outside of town on Route 127 North and you reach the recently renovated **Emerson Inn**, Cape Ann's grand hotel, well situated for dinner in Rockport and perhaps a show at the contemporary Shalin Liu Performance Center. Just up the road is **Halibut Point State Park**. Get out of the car to visit the large quarry in the center of the park, now filled rainwater. Then take the wide gravel path past countless large boulders that line the shoreline for a wide-ranging vista of the coastline north to Plum Island.

Continue on 127 North to find the small seaside community of Annisquam and then take Route 133 West to reach Essex. If it's anywhere near lunch or dinner time, you'll no doubt spot a long line out the door at the legendary seafood shack, **Woodman's**, the place where the fried clam was reportedly first created on July 3, 1916. Around the bend on Route 133, you'll reach the home of **Essex River Basin Adventures**, an outfitter that offers exhilarating two-hour guided kayaking tours through the web of estuaries in the Essex Marsh.

To find your own spit of sand on 4-mile-long Crane Beach, turn right on Argilla Road before reaching the historic town of Ipswich. Pull over just before the beach at Russell Orchards. In operation since 1920, you'll find just-baked cider doughnuts, muffins, apple cider, hard cider, and fruit-flavored wine. In summer, you can head out into the fields to pick-your-own strawberries and apples. Also visit the impressive grounds of the **Crane Estate** next door to the beach to roam the half-mile long Grand Allée that leads from the Great House to the sea. This is Massachusetts' version of Versailles.

The Maine Moose Run, Rangeley to Kingfield, Maine

The Maine interior is one of the most undeveloped regions in the northeast, a blanket of forest filled with mile-high mountains traversed by the Appalachian Trail, colossal lakes, long rivers such as the Kennebago and Penobscot, and too many ponds to count. Many Mainers consider the small village of Rangeley, the main hub of the Rangeley Lakes Region, as the gateway to this vast tract of land. Several summers ago, Rangeley hosted a Maine Moose Calling Contest. That moose call may come in handy when you drive out of town on Route 16 north to Stratton, where moose are regularly spotted at dawn or dusk.

In Stratton, head south on Route 27 to Carrabassett Valley, home to Sugarloaf Mountain Resort and the **Sugarloaf Outdoor Center**. Rent bikes and venture onto their vast network of trails that loop around lonely ponds and along streams, always with broad-shouldered Sugarloaf Mountain in the background. Expert bikers can tackle the newly cut Oak Knoll Trail which makes its ascent some 600 feet up to your lodging for the night, **Stratton Brook Hut**, the latest property to be built by Maine Huts & Trails. Hikers can make the 90-minute climb under the tall pines on Newton's Revenge Trail. Once at the hut, reward yourself with a Baxter Stowaway IPA and stroll over to "The Vista." A bench looks out on a wide swath of uninterrupted wilderness that includes the Bigelow Range, 4,000-foot peaks that form the backbone of a ridge walk on the Appalachian Trail.

Back at the trailhead, continue on to Kingfield for a requisite burrito stop at **Rolling Fatties**. Then you can loop back to Rangeley or head an hour north to The Forks to go white-water rafting on the Kennebago River. If you want to put that moose call to work once again, head 90 minutes north of Kingfield to Greenville and Moosehead Lake, home to their signature Moose Cruise.

Shoot the Gaps, Warren to Middlebury, Vermont

In Vermont, they call them the gaps, narrow roads that cut through the otherwise impassable ridge of the Green Mountains, offering astounding vistas and providing backcountry access to the Long Trail, the state-long hiking route. Begin in Warren at the **Pitcher Inn**, where more than 40 local artists combined their talents to give this Relais & Chateaux property a distinct Vermont feel. Then drive west on the Lincoln Gap and rise to the top of the crest where you'll find a parking lot on the left hand side of the road. Continue on foot on the Long Trail, heading south, and a little over one mile later, you'll reach Sunset Ledge. Views of the Adirondacks can be seen to the west, past the rolling tapestry of farmland and meadows. Just to your north in the Green Mountains is the 4,017-foot peak of Mount Abraham. Get back in the car and head downhill into Lincoln and onward to Bristol and Middlebury on Routes 16 and 7 South. Here, you'll find stately college buildings and a rare Pulp Mill double-barreled covered bridge.

Continue on Route 7 South to Route 125 East to reach Ripton, start of the Middlebury Gap and once home to poet laureate, Robert Frost. For 39 years, he would summer in a log cabin lost in the hillside. The mile-long Robert Frost Interpretive Trail is a good introduction to his work, ambling through the forest while reading seven Frost poems on signs. Continue your drive upward for more glorious views of the mountain wilderness. Once you reach the farming community of Hancock, take a left turn on Route 100 North to complete the loop back in Warren.

Life's a Beach, My Top 12 Picks

Whether you crave the shallow waters of the Long Island Sound, the rolling dunes of the Cape Cod National Seashore, or the jagged granite shores of Maine's long inlets, the New England coast is a multi-faceted mecca for sun worshippers. The only problem is finding that pristine speck of sand that has yet to be covered with a towel. Heading from warm water to cold water (south to north), here's a guide to those beloved beaches folks venture to when the crowds become too hot to handle.

Compo Beach, Westport, Connecticut

Yes, the weekend price might be prohibitive at $30 weekdays, $50 weekends per car, but the white sands of Westport, Connecticut's Compo Beach is by far the best slice of paradise within an hour drive of Manhattan. The long sweeping beach has its fair share of seashells as you stroll down to the warm waters of the Sound. There's also a wooden playground with small turrets and tunnels for kids to roam in.

Hammonasset Beach, Madison, Connecticut

I'm a sand hog, I admit it. I like to stretch out on my own slice of paradise with a beach towel, chairs, books and magazine, and goodies to eat. That's why I savor the space of the 2-mile long stretch of shoreline at Hammonasset. I park my car near the East

Bathhouse and walk a short way on the soft white sand toward Meigs Point. Backed by grassy dunes and wildflowers, the shallow strip of sand is so long it never feels crowded, even on a hot weekend day in summer. I read, swim in the blue-green waters of the Sound, peer off at the lighthouse, read some more, bite into fresh fruit, and always wander over to the Meigs Point Nature Center with the kids. We feel the crabs in the Touch Tank, see the native snakes and turtles, and walk through the butterfly garden. Then it's back to my towel to stretch out as far as I can.

East Beach, Charlestown, Rhode Island

You want a place of solace and repose. Somewhere to bring that big thick novel and listen to the sounds of surf meeting sand. You need a day on the sugar white sands of East Beach. This three-mile long barrier beach separates Block Island Sound from Ninigret Pond. While there is little shade, the ever-present breeze is perfect on a hot summer's day. Your placid retreat is enhanced by the sweet smell of rambling beach roses, whose pink blossoms provide the best form of aromatherapy.

Second Beach, Middletown, Rhode Island

Everyone rides the waves at Second Beach, located just outside the Newport town line. Surfers are found to the right of the beach, near Purgatory Chasm, a deep cleft in the bedrock that rises above Sachuest Bay. Atop the cliffs is the campus of St. George's School and the tall brick chapel that forms a dramatic backdrop from the powdery sand. Families grab their boogie boards and head to the center of the beach to try their luck. Singles and college kids can usually be found to the left, using their body to ride the crest. Everyone comes for the surf, which pounds the shores with its consistent thump. It also helps that the waters of Rhode Island are warmer than the beaches of Cape Ann and Cape Cod, so Bostonians think nothing of making the hour-long drive south. After swallowing gulps of the Atlantic, the crowds retreat to the spacious shoreline, only to jump back in the ocean when their bodies wilt under the relentless sun.

Nauset Light Beach, Eastham, Massachusetts

40 miles of windswept sand dunes, kettle hole ponds, bogs, scrub forest, and marshes combine to form the serene Cape Cod National Seashore. As logic dictates, the farther out you go, the fewer crowds you'll contend with. I like to bike to Nauset Light Beach in the early morning when the fog still casts a hazy glaze over the water. I walk down the sand path to the soft white beach, joined by surfers, dog walkers. Then I take my first glance back at the towering tan colored dunes, realizing instantly why JFK wanted this landscape to be preserved as a National Seashore. Looking to the left as the beach curves toward Wellfleet, the dunes meld with sand, sea, and sky, as if the land is going to plummet into the water. Listen to the waves, watch the surfers glide atop the ocean, see the seals popping their heads out of the water like periscopes, walk the beach to find an errant lobster trap run ashore, and savor the scene before families start to pour in around 11 am.

South Beach, Martha's Vineyard, Massachusetts

Take the 4-mile bike trail from Edgartown to South Beach and you'll be ready to go for a dip. Sloping down to the sea, South Beach, a favorite of the locals, with a wild, blustery feel to it. And it's easy to carve your own spot out of this 3-mile-long stretch of sand. Afterwards, venture to nearby Katama Airfield and have lunch at **The Right Fork Diner**. The children will enjoy watching the biplanes take flight overhead.

Surfside Beach, Nantucket, Massachusetts

Accessibility, with or without a car, is key to being a thriving teenager hangout. In that popular family vacation destination of Nantucket, all teenagers need to do is rent a bike in town and pedal an easy 3 miles on a bike path to reach Surfside Beach. Big groups hit the waves, singles hang at the snack bar, and those with a need for privacy head to either end of the beach.

Crane Beach, Ipswich, Massachusetts

It's easy to find your own spit of sand at Crane Beach, where the white crescent beach spans more than four miles. Tours of the Crane Estate's Great House, designed by architect David Adler, are offered by the Trustees from late May through October. Also visit the impressive grounds, including the half-mile long Grand Allée that leads from the Great House to the sea. The Trustees recently replanted many of the spruce trees that line this green boulevard.

Wingaersheek Beach, Gloucester, Massachusetts

Wingaersheek's shallow waters are a family favorite for Bostonians. At low tide you can walk close to a mile to that gleaming white lighthouse jutting out from the tip of land at Annisquam. When the water rushes in, indentations in the sand make ideal warm wading pools for toddlers who may be wary of ocean waves. The older kids love the large rock formations on either side of the beach, where you can clamber up and down the boulders, looking for crabs.

Odiorne Point State Park, Rye, New Hampshire

The granite state extends to the rock littered shoreline of Odiorne Point, just south of Portsmouth. Yet, there is one sandy stretch of beach in Odiorne that offers a quintessential New England seascape. That includes one of the most picturesque lighthouses along the Eastern Seaboard, the circa-1872 granite Whaleback, the historic Wentworth by the Sea lodging, a long breakwater, and all those sailboats heading in and out of the dark blue Atlantic. The hard part is finding this hidden gem. I always park my car at the boat launch and then bike on the trail along Route 1A towards the main parking lot. Less than a half-mile later, a wide grassy dirt road leads through the forest of Odiorne all the way to the breakwater called Frost Point. The dense sand slopes to the water's edge just to the left of Frost Point, a placid retreat with less than a handful of people in the know reclining on their beach chairs. And you thought all New Hampshire beaches were crowded?

Footbridge Beach, Ogunquit, Maine

At Ogunquit's 3-mile-long Main Beach in southern Maine, sunbathers are packed like sardines in summer. To escape this swarming mass of civilization, head two miles north on Ocean Street and turn right to reach the Footbridge Beach parking lot. The gently lapping waves and the expansive stretch of sand are ideal for families.

Popham Beach, Phippsburg, Maine

At the end of one of those fingers of land that dangles off the Maine coast into the Atlantic, Popham is hopelessly exposed to all the elements. There's nothing manicured about this rare spit of sand sandwiched between the rocky shores. Pieces of driftwood lie on the beach, backed by dwarf pines and uprooted trees. Come at low tide and the grooved sand leads to a tiny island where seagulls have picked over unfortunate crabs and mussels that lay exposed on the kelp. When the water rolls in, kids swim in the warm (yes, warm) waters of the tidal pool as parents take long beach walks, watching three-masted schooners and lobstermen cruise past the pine-studded islands and lighthouses. Let the cool breeze blow through your hair and breathe in the salty air. This is the raw, genuine Maine coast you have yearned for.

10 Most Instagrammable Sites, Including Night Sky and Sunsets

Lobster Buoys on the Docks of Cape Porpoise, Maine

The Boulder Strewn Coastline of Prouts Neck, Maine

Portland Head Light, Portland, Maine

Peering Down at Somes Sounds from Atop Acadia Mountain, Acadia National Park, Maine

AMC Lakes of the Clouds Hut for Stargazing, The White Mountains, New Hampshire

The Village Green at Craftsbury Common, Vermont

Bash Bish Falls, Mount Washington, Massachusetts

Gay Head Cliffs (Aquinnah) at Martha's Vineyard, Massachusetts

Herring Cove Beach at Sunset, Provincetown, Massachusetts

The Cliff Walk behind the Mansions of Newport, Rhode Island

3 Ways to Savor Lighthouses

Aboard the J. & E. Riggin, Sailing from Rockland, ME

There are over 60 lighthouses on the Maine coast and approximately one-third of those lighthouses can be found in Penobscot Bay, the cruising grounds for the circa-1927 Maine windjammer J. & E. Riggin. Hop aboard for one of their 4-day Maine Lighthouses and Lobster Cruises throughout the summer and you'll be clicking picturesque photo after photo. Captain Annie Mahle, author of the cookbook, At Home, At Sea, is known for her innovative and tasty fare. So expect your lobster to be served atop a bed of sun-dried tomato fettuccini, served with fresh baked biscuits. Save room for desserts like butter-scotch-topped gingerbread with sautéed apples.

On a Stroll Around Portland Head Light, Cape Elizabeth, Maine

Built in 1791 and sitting on a bluff perched out to sea, the exquisite white edifice of the Portland Head Light has been painted by the likes of Edward Hopper. Though it's the boulder-strewn coastline Winslow Homer depicted so brilliantly that comes to mind when walking along the rocky shoreline at Fort Williams Park. Both artists appreciated Maine in the off-season, when crowds were at a minimum. Stroll around the entirety of Portland Head Light, taking in its 80-foot height. On rare occasions, the lighthouse is open for a quick climb to the top. Then hit the trails that line the shoreline. Lobstermen haul up traps from the back of their boats, while farther out to sea, oil tankers make their way in and out of Portland Harbor. If you were wise, you booked at least one night's stay at the nearby Inn by the Sea, where you can dine on fresh Maine seafood at night and walk the adjacent beach during the day. (Please also see the entry, "Bike to 5 Lighthouses in Portland with Summer Feet Cycling" in the **5 Authentic Guided Day Trips** chapter on page 178).

The Perfect Place to Picnic, Great Point, Nantucket, Massachusetts

The only company you'll have on a stroll to Nantucket's Great Point are birds. The rolling dunes and brush on this narrow strip of land are the nesting grounds of the endangered piping plover. Hike around the Great Point Lighthouse, a partially solar-powered replica of the 1818 original, and you're also likely to find marsh hawks, ospreys, and the playful American oystercatcher. That orange carrot sticking out of his mouth is actually his beak. Nearby, the **Wauwinet Resort** will drive you out to Great Point, even provide the fare for a romantic escape.

3 Ways to Savor Covered Bridges

Bike Through the Covered Bridges of Waitsfield and Warren, Vermont

A 15-mile loop skirts the mountains and enters Waitsfield and Warren via covered bridges. Start your ride at the junction of Route 100 and Route 17, turning onto the shoulder of Route 100 South. Considering the high peaks of Lincoln, Ellen, and Abraham to your right, the road is remarkably flat. At 5.4 miles, take a sharp left onto Covered Bridge Road. Constructed in 1880, the wooden bridge spans the Mad River. Turn left and ride through the village of Warren, making a point to stop at the Warren Store for lunch. Take your next right onto Brook Road and climb into Lincoln Valley. Dairy farms, green meadows, and fields of corn stand at the side of the now East Warren Road. The slopes of Sugarbush appear to your left and a rare round barn, the centerpiece of the **Inn at Round Barn** (and now used as an indoor pool) can be seen to your right. From here, you cruise downhill all the way to the covered bridge in Waitsfield, built in 1833.

Dine with View of a Covered Bridge, Quechee, Vermont

One of my favorite restaurants in Vermont is just outside Woodstock, the **Simon Pearce restaurant** in

Quechee. Simon Pearce is best known for his glass-ware and you can visit his store and see glassblowers at work downstairs in this former mill. But it's the restaurant, with spectacular views of water tumbling down the rocks in front of a covered bridge, that brings me back almost every time I'm in the state. Reserve one of the tables near the window, get here on the early side for dinner, before it gets too dark, and you're in for a treat. The food is secondary to the view and the sturdy glassware you'll use, created by Simon Pearce.

Drive through 4 Covered Bridges, Swanzey, New Hampshire

The southwest corner of New Hampshire is a rela-tively flat section of woods, farmland, college towns, and most notably, covered bridges. These wooden relics of yesteryear still stand as testament to simpler times. This 18-mile route loops through four of the covered bridges on quiet country roads. To access this route from Keene, take State Route 12 South to State Route 32 South to Swanzey. At the junction of State Route 32 and Sawyers Crossing Road, start at Monadnock Regional High School. Head south on State Route 32 for 1.5 miles till you reach Carlton Road. Turn left and you'll soon pass through covered bridge Numero Uno. First built in 1869, the Carlton Road Bridge uses a lattice of X-shaped wooden crosses to hold the ceiling in place. 1.1 miles from the junction of State Route 32 and Carlton Road, turn right at the T-junction onto Webber Hill Road. You'll swing downhill past the East Swanzey Post Office, where you'll meet up with State Route 32 again. Veer right for 0.1 mile to Swanzey Lake Road where you turn left. This 3.9-mile ride brings you past Swanzey Lake. For views of the water, turn right onto West Shore Drive; otherwise, continue straight between the houses, farms, and small towns to Westport Road. Turn left and ride 0.8 mile to a stop sign on Main Street. Another left will bring you to the junction of Route 10. Veer left for a mere 0.3 mile to reach Coombs Road, where you turn right for covered bridge number two. Built in 1837, the 118-foot Coombs Bridge spans the Ashuelot River.

Retrace your trail back to Main Street, turn right and go for 0.7 mile, bearing right again on Westport Road for an additional 2.4 miles. This brings you to a three-way stop at the intersection of Christian Hill Road. Turn left through the quaint village of West Swanzey to reach my favorite bridge on the trip, the Thompson Bridge. One of the two sidewalks still remain from the original construction (1832). To reach the final bridge, turn right on Winchester Road immediately after the Thompson Bridge. At the junction of Route 10, turn right for 0.6 mile and be cautious of the traffic. A right turn on Sawyers Crossing Road will eventually bring you to Sawyers Crossing Bridge, the longest of the four bridges. Continue straight to a stop sign and turn left on Eaton Road. This will bring you back to the high school.

5 Quintessential New England Towns

Want to see the New England of yore, where few things ever change? Try these towns as starters:

East Burke, Vermont

Head to East Burke and you'll be embraced by a blanket of greenery, where century old barns and their fresh coats of red paint form a striking contrast to the velvety meadows that blow in the summer breeze. It's no surprise that this unvarnished chunk of northeastern Vermont has become a mecca for the outdoors lover who yearns to breathe in the fragrant pines while strolling or biking the countryside. East Burke has all the necessary establishments for a memorable rural escape—several B&Bs, a country store, a restaurant that takes pride in serving Vermont's finest summer produce, and a bike store. Yet, the small town refuses to be overrun by commercialism like other ski areas in the state. Head to Darling Hill Road, where the huge barns that once housed the Jersey cows and Morgan horses of Elmer Darling at the turn of last century are now part of the Inn at Mountain View Farm.

Jackson, New Hampshire

Blink and you'll miss the turn-off on Route 16 to reach Jackson and what a pity that would be. Venture through that covered bridge to enter another era, one where serenity and stunning scenery merge to create an ideal escape from modernity any time of year. The circular green of Jackson, ringed by inns, antique stores, and cafes, has been thriving as a resort town since the mid-nineteenth century. But don't expect any honky-tonk. That's down the road in North Conway. Jackson is a peaceful respite in the heart of the Presidential Range. Peer up from the Jackson green and the panorama of White Mountain peaks is mesmerizing.

Kennebunkport, Maine

Most people associate Kennebunkport with the shopping at Dock Square. That's a shame. The true joy of visiting Kennebunkport is driving on back-country roads to find the lobster traps stocked high on Cape Porpoise, the small strip of sand at Goose Rocks Beach, and the many favorite local eateries in between like **Nunan's Lobster Hut** or **The Ramp**. For a memorable dining experience, reserve a table at the venerable **White Barn Inn**.

Madison, Connecticut

Even on a hot weekend day in summer, the 2-mile-long stretch of beach at Hammonasset never feels too crowded. Park your car near the East Bathhouse and walk a short way on the soft white sand toward Meigs Point. Backed by grassy dunes and wildflowers, this is the perfect welcome mat to the blue-green waters of the Long Island Sound. After you finish that big thick novel, drive 5 minutes to the charming village of Madison. Coffee shops, restaurants, and boutique stores entice the beachgoer, but you'd be wise to find your next good read at one of the finest bookstores in New England, **RJ Julia Independent Booksellers**.

Little Compton, Rhode Island

Best known for its historic village common and centuries-old cemetery, Little Compton also boasts a gem of a beach just down the road. Backed by a salt marsh, crescent-shaped Goosewing Beach is managed by The Nature Conservancy and is just as popular with walkers as sunbathers. Grab your quahog chowder and johnnycakes at The Common's Lunch (48 Commons) after your day of breathing in the salty air.

For the Outdoor Lover

7 Best Bike Rides

New England's diversity of terrain, history, and compact size have all helped to create one of the top road biking destinations in the country. The main attraction being the stunning scenery—the white steeples that dot the rolling green hills and farmland of Vermont, the sweeping mounds of sand that form Cape Cod, the rocky coast of Maine, and the Atlantic islands with their moors, bogs, and beaches. These are the rides that stand out for me:

Block Island, Rhode Island

Most people associate Rhode Island with the palatial estates that sit on the southern end of Aquidneck Island in a town called Newport. Well, Block Island is the antithesis of materialism, a wild sliver of land 12 miles south of the mainland that has taken advantage of its remote setting to preserve its natural beauty. Strict zoning laws prohibit modernity from creeping into the charm and luster of Block Island's bygone era. The hour ferry ride from Galilee leaves you on a pork chop-shaped island where weathered houses brave the ocean's wrath atop hillsides, bordered by old stone walls and blue-green ponds. Add that rugged coastline to the equation and you have a scene that feels more like the Scottish Highlands than New England.

Orient yourself with a lovely 13-mile bike ride around the island. You'll be disembarking in Old

Harbor, the only town on the island. Turn left and continue past a statue, biking in a clockwise manner. Almost immediately after leaving town, small fields cropped with cedar shingle houses appear on the right, the vast ocean to the left. Cruising uphill, the Southeast Lighthouse stands tall over the sea. Indeed, it's on the highest ground of any lighthouse in New England. The original lens of eight fisheye panels made of French crystal cost $10,000 in 1880. Today, it would cost more than $10 million. Stroll around the lighthouse and then walk over to the Mohegan Bluffs parking lot. A trail lined with bayberry bushes and rose hips (when the rose hips turn red, people use it to make tea) leads to those majestic Mohegan cliffs. Another path leads down to a beach where you can feel inconsequential as you walk below massive sheets of rock.

Exchange two legs for two wheels and turn left through a series of small ponds covered with lily pads. Ride past Center Road to Cooneymus Road and look for a sign to Rodman's Hollow, a deep cleft in the land a half-mile wide that goes right down to the sea. Then pedal toward the southwestern part of the island, turning left at the sign for Chaplin's Marina. Situated on Great Salt Pond's New Harbor, you'll see sailors getting their boats in ship shape to head out on the water. At Corn Neck Road, turn left to ride along the moors that line Block Island's most popular beach, Crescent. This 3-mile stretch of sand is packed with day-trippers in the summer months. From here, it's an easy ride back to Old Harbor.

Little Compton, Rhode Island

South of Route 195 and the gritty mill towns of Fall River and New Bedford lies countryside so fertile you'll feel like you're in Vermont. Stretching from Dartmouth, Massachusetts, to Little Compton, Rhode Island, the area is known as the Heritage Farm Coast. It has the sunniest and most temperate climate in New England and thus the longest growing season. Dairy farms, corn fields, even vineyards, border the Sakonnet River as it washes into the Atlantic.

For a good 20-mile loop, take Route 77 south from Tiverton Four Corners to Sakonnet Point and return on backcountry roads past the village green of Little Compton. Tiverton Four Corners is a rural village that dates from the 17th century and is now home to artisans like jeweler **Tiffany Peay** (3851 Main Road), who uses brightly colored gems to create bracelets and necklaces with contemporary flair. Or energize with an ice cream cone at the legendary **Gray's** (16 East Road), which serves my favorite black raspberry in New England. The stretch of road heading south from Tiverton Four Corners is a beaut, with views of rolled hay leading to the shores of the wide Sakonnet River. When you finally reach Little Compton, you've earned those Johnnycakes (fried cornmeal) at The Common's Lunch. But first, get a feel for the history of this quintessential New England village by walking across the street to the white steeple, village green, and cemetery. Stubs stick out of the ground and if you peer closely, you'll notice that the first settlers are buried here, with dates of death registered as far back as 1711.

Westport, Massachusetts

Turn left out of the Westport Middle School parking lot onto Old Country Road to start this 21-mile loop (give yourself at least two hours). A right turn onto Pine Hill Road heads downhill, but the route is relatively flat for most of the ride. Within a mile, you're lost in acres of farmland. Historic Cape Cod shingled houses and barns are bordered by old stone walls. Continue on lightly traveled Old Pine Road to see row upon row of corn edging out onto the horizon. A mile later, turn right onto Hix Bridge Road and then left a half-mile beyond that onto Horseneck Road. The Westport River appears on your right, a strip of dark blue snaking through the emerald green pasture. If you take this ride in the summer, you can purchase produce straight from the farmers—blueberries, sweet corn, tomatoes, whatever the farm happens to be harvesting at the time.

Around the halfway mark, the ocean starts to appear on your left and the area becomes more developed. A good choice for lunch is the **Bayside**, known for their cod wraps and lobster rolls. Veer right on East Beach Road for expansive views of the ocean. Another right onto Route 88 leads to the sweeping beach and dunes of Horseneck Beach State Reservation, a great spot to take a dip. After crossing a small bridge which rewards you with views of the harbor and its numerous fishing boats, turn right onto Drift Road. This leads to Old County Road, where you turn left to return to your car.

Provincetown, Massachusetts

Cape Cod is blessed with a bevy of paved bike trails, from the Shining Sea Bikeway that extends from Falmouth to Woods Hole, to the Cape Cod Canal Bike Path that snakes under the Sagamore and Bourne Bridges. Then there's the popular 22-mile Cape Cod Rail Trail that meanders through the middle of the Cape from South Dennis to Wellfleet. Many bike trails, like the CCRT are former railroad lines with little or no grade. If you have a hankering for hills (not to mention ocean views), head to the 8-mile-long Province Lands Bike Trail at the tip of the Cape. The rollercoaster route dips in and out of sand dunes, weaving through scrub-pine forests and along beaches in one of the most unique bike paths you'll ever ride. The loop starts at Herring Cove Beach and heads inland through Beech Forest, where the trees are often home to colorful warblers. Before sweeping downhill to the Province Lands Visitors Center, stop and look at the mounds of sand as they roll to the ocean. The Cape Cod National Seashore at its finest.

Nantucket, Massachusetts

Biking is my favorite mode of travel in Nantucket. If I'm craving a long ride by myself, I head east from old Nantucket town (where the ferries arrive) through the moors and cranberry bogs until I arrive at the rose-trellised cottages of Sconset. If I'm with the family, I'll opt for an easy 3-mile bike trail to the waves of Surfside Beach. Kid-free, my wife and I savor a late afternoon pedal to Madaket Beach. On the westernmost tip of Nantucket, Madaket's beach has a narrow, wild feel to it as the white sand quickly drops down to the waters of the Atlantic. We bring a backpack full of provisions, say fresh sushi from **Bar Yoshi** (21 Old South Wharf), plop ourselves on the beach (preferably after 6 pm when most families have vanished), and get ready to savor the sunset. Wine could help bring on that blissful From Here to Eternity moment of rolling in the waves, but we know full well that it's a 5-mile jaunt on a rolling path back into town. So a bottle of seltzer water with lime might be the more pragmatic choice.

Addison, Vermont

Biking outfitters have pounced on Vermont like miners on a vein of gold. And why not? The state's pastoral setting is ideally suited to the sport. Lightly traveled backcountry roads are rarely used outside of a handful of dairy farmers who live and work there. Around every bend, there's another meadow greener than the last, another anonymous mountain standing tall in the distance, another quintessential New England village where a freshly painted white steeple pierces the clouds overhead.

Start your ride near the shores of Lake Champlain in Addison. Heading north on Lake Road, you're smack dab in a fertile breadbasket. To your right are glimpses of stacked hay, lounging cows, corn that has already been reaped, tall silos, and the spine of the Green Mountains. On your left are the waters of Lake Champlain, with the colorful Adirondack Mountains rising from the opposite shores. Continue straight through a thicket of pines on Arnold Bay Road, where

Benedict Arnold held his ground on this site to win a major battle against the British in the Revolutionary War, and soon you'll cross Otter Creek to reach the town of Vergennes. As you head south on the return trip, the route turns into a rollicking good ride up and down the hillside past a quilt of patchwork farms and the smell of Vermont best form of aromatherapy, manure.

Islesboro, Maine

Of all the Penobscot Bay Islands that dot the waters of Maine, Islesboro is arguably the best for biking. The terrain is relatively flat, yet hilly enough to offer majestic views of the bay, and long enough to offer a 28-mile bike ride. Once you disembark from the 20-minute ferry ride from Lincolnville, turn right and pedal past the million-dollar mansions of Dark Harbor (so-called "summer cottages") on the way south to Pendleton Point. Here, the perennial battering of the surf has taken its toll on the beach. Long, striated rocks look like rotted tree trunks. Harbor seals and loons might be lounging in the water when you take a snack break on the boulders (purchased at the lone general store in Dark Harbor). Turning around, the road narrows at Islesboro Harbor, offering mountainous views of Camden Hills State Park to the left and the wide open Atlantic to the right.

10 Classic New England Hikes

If your daily path is an exhaust-sucking, construction-dodging trial, then it's time to get off the pavement and get lost in the woods. There's nothing like a good climb to replenish your lungs with oxygen-rich air. Use common sense and stick to the appropriate level of difficulty and you'll make it back to your car rejuvenated. If you haven't climbed a mountain since Pedro was pitching for the Red Sox, don't start with Katahdin. Even the hikes listed as easy will challenge anyone who has not strolled uphill in a while. But once you reach the top, covered in sweat, and surrounded by a carpet of pines, it makes it all worthwhile.

Mount Monadnock, Jaffrey Center, New Hampshire

For many New England children, their first mountain climb is up that broad-shouldered peak Henry David Thoreau called a "sublime mass," Mt. Monadnock. Just over the border of Massachusetts in southern New Hampshire, Monadnock is less than a two-hour drive from Boston. Its accessibility and locale, smack dab in the center of New England, has made it the second most popular mountain ascent in the world (averaging about 130,000 climbers a year). Only Mt. Fuji in Japan has more foot traffic. Head up the White Dot trail, one of the steepest ascents to the peak, but also one that rewards with you with incredible vistas in a very short time. Above tree-line, the forest recedes to form open ledges covered with low-lying shrubs like mountain cranberry bushes. This gives you ample opportunity to rest and peer down at the Currier and Ives setting below—a soft blanket of treetops, small towns, a smattering of lakes and ponds, and farms that fan out to anonymous ridges. Soon you'll reach the 3,165-foot summit, where Thoreau watched in dismay as his fellow mid-19th century trampers inscribed their names in rock. This didn't stop him from writing in large letters atop the biggest boulder "H.D.T. Ate Gorp Here, 1860." I'm joking, but you can see many other names clearly marked like "T.S. Spaulding, 1853."

3 to 4 hours. Moderate. Follow State Route 124 West through Jaffrey Center and look for the signs for the Monadnock State Park headquarters. The trailhead is located in the front of the visitor center.

Falling Waters/Old Bridle Path Loop, Franconia Notch State Park, New Hampshire

The strenuous climb up Mt. Lafayette is worthy of all the accolades hikers bestow upon it. With tumbling waterfalls, a steep ascent to three of the highest peaks in New England, and a 1.7-mile ridge walk where the spruce-studded White Mountains stand below you in a dizzying display of green, this very well could be the finest day hike in New England. Turn into the woods from the parking lot, and I-93's traffic is quickly replaced by the sounds of rushing water, compliments of a stream that accompanies you for a good mile and a half. Three perfect falls swirl over smooth boulders to pools of water the color of gin, the ideal stop for a breather. You'll need your energy to get to the top of Little Haystack Mountain and the start of the Franconia Ridge Trail. Part of the Appalachian Trail, this above-tree-line path offers a stunning panorama of New England's highest summits, including Mount Washington. Bag 5,108-foot Mount Lincoln and 5,249-foot Mount Lafayette before taking the Greenleaf Trail down the boulder littered slopes to AMC's Greenleaf Hut. This deep-woods stop is great for lemonade refills and catching up on the latest trail gossip.

6 to 8 hours. Strenuous. From Woodstock, New Hampshire, take I-93 North to the Falling Waters/ Bridle Path parking lot.

Mount Willard, Crawford Notch, New Hampshire

If the thought of climbing a mountain makes you sweat long before leaving your car, wipe your brow and give 2,804-foot Willard a try. In less than an hour, you'll make it to the peak where jaw-dropping views of Crawford Notch stand below you, a reward for your slight efforts. Not surprisingly, this easy climb is a favorite for families. The hike begins behind the Crawford Notch Visitor Center, former site of the Crawford railroad station. The trail starts off sharply but becomes more gradual as you criss-cross through a forest of dense pines. Eventually, sunshine seeps into the woods and you'll reach a large opening, the light at the end of the tunnel. Look down from the rocky ledge at the old railroad line, carved into the mountainside, and the onslaught of cars that snake through Crawford Notch on Route 302. Then pat yourself on the back for climbing a White Mountain.

1 to 2 hours. Easy. From North Conway, take Route 16 North to U.S. 302 West up though Crawford Notch. Park at the Crawford Notch Visitor Center just next to the AMC hut.

Welch/Dickey Mountain Trail, Waterville Valley, New Hampshire

The short summits of Welch and Dickey Mountains offer such grand vistas that it's not uncommon to find wedding parties atop this trail. That's not to say this 4.5-mile loop is easy. The bride usually foregoes her traditional wedding dress for T-shirt, shorts, and hiking boots.

The trail leaves the parking area and enters a forest of beeches, maples, and oaks, before turning sharply to the right to reach the southern ridge of Welch Mountain. A little over a mile later, you're on an exposed ledge, looking down at sylvan Waterville Valley and the miniature cars weaving their way through the mountains on Route 49. Unfortunately, this is not the top. The summit is another 0.7 mile up boulders where twisted jack pines and dwarf birches have been stunted by their exposure to harsh winters. The 2,605-foot peak is a good place to stop and have lunch. Then proceed to the summit of Dickey Mountain (2,734 feet). Back at the bottom, make sure to toast the bride and catch her bouquet.

3 hours. Easy to Moderate. Take Exit 28 off I-93 and go east on Route 49 towards Waterville Valley.

Turn left approximately 6 miles later, crossing a bridge and following Upper Mad River Road for 0.7 mile. At Orris Road, turn right and go 0.6 mile to the parking lot.

Maiden Cliff, Camden, Maine

North of the country of Brazil, the shoreline on the Atlantic seaboard remains flat until one arrives at Camden Hills State Park. Maine's mid-coast mountains reward hikers with views of the Atlantic, three-masted schooners sailing in the open waters, and picturesque harbors like the one in Camden. All for one or two hours of effort. The Maiden Cliff trail strolls through hemlocks until you reach a junction at the half-mile mark. Turn right onto Ridge Trail and soon the ledges open up onto the waters of Megunticook Lake. The view only gets better when you turn left at the aptly named Scenic Trail and continue to the summit. The Penobscot Bay islands of Islesboro and North Haven can be seen in the distance. Follow the white blazes and several hundred yards later, you'll find a huge white cross. This marks the spot where 12-year-old Elenora French plunged to her death on May 7, 1864. She was running to catch her hat. This might be the fastest way down, but not recommended.

2 hours. Easy. From Camden, take Route 52 West, 3 miles from the intersection of Route 1. There will be a small parking area on the right-hand side of the road just before Route 52 borders the lake.

Gulf Hagas, Brownville Junction, Maine.

When a raging river drops precipitously through narrow canyon walls, the result is a series of frothy waterfalls and swimming holes so frigid that only a native Mainer could dip his head. Smack dab in the Hundred Mile Wilderness Region, the 8-mile Gulf Hagas hike is a remote wilderness gem. A 45-minute drive on dirt roads from Greenville, Gulf Hagas is a gorge carved by the pounding waters of the Pleasant River and lumbermen's dynamite. A series of exquisite waterfalls await you as the river drops nearly 500 feet in 2.5 miles through the narrow walls of the slate canyon. You should give yourself at least seven hours to enjoy the entire loop. Extended roots, large boulders, and sheets of rock make walking slow and you'll want to stop numerous times to take in the views and swim. Buttermilk Falls is an apt name for the frothy white foam the water becomes as it churns down the rocks. A swimming hole just beyond the falls is a favorite place for hikers to strip down to their undergarments and plunge into the auburn-red waters. Those piercing screams heard are just folks getting used to the icy temperature.

7 hours, Moderate. 4 miles north of Brownville Junction on Route 11, turn left at the sign for Katahdin Iron Works. Drive 6.5 miles to the Works, where you register and pay a day-fee to the logging company. Also ask for a map. At the fork, bear right and then left 3.4 miles later. Approximately 7 miles from the Works, you'll see a large parking lot.

Mount Katahdin, Baxter State Park, Maine

Katahdin is a fitting end to the Appalachian Trail in the north. Reaching the mass of rock atop the 5,267-foot summit is a challenge to the most experienced climber, even the AT thru-hiker who spent the last six months racking up more than 2,100 miles. Yet, it's somewhat of a disappointment that the AT ascends Katahdin from the Hunt Trail, the easiest (if there's such a thing) and least spectacular path to the peak. For an unparalleled mountainous ascent in the northeast, you should opt for the Knife Edge. Like the name implies, this three to foot wide granite sidewalk sharply drops off more than 1,500 feet on either side. The best way to reach the Knife Edge is the Helen Taylor Trail from the Roaring Brook Campground. All the ascents are a struggle. You start at about 1,500 feet and don't stop climbing until you run out of mountain. When the Helen Taylor trail hits Pamola Peak, a little over three miles into the climb, bear left to find the Knife Edge. First you'll ascend South Peak, then Baxter Peak, the summit of Katahdin. Rest those spaghetti legs and take in the exquisite vistas of northern Maine—Chesuncook Lake, the West Branch of the Penobscot River, Big and Little Spencer Mountains, and all the peaks that form massive Katahdin. As you gloat, proud of your grand accomplishment, just remember that Henry David Thoreau climbed Katahdin without a trail. "It was vast, Titanic, such as man never inhabits. Some part of the beholder, even some vital part, seems to escape through the loose grating of his ribs as he ascends," Thoreau noted in The Maine Woods. No doubt, you'll agree.

8 to 10 hours. Strenuous. The trailhead is located at the Roaring Brook Campground, 8 miles north of the Togue Pond Gatehouse in Baxter State Park. Arrive by 6:30 am since the parking lot fills up rapidly and hikers are then turned away.

Mount Pisgah, West Burke, Vermont

Arriving at Lake Willoughby from the south, the dark blue waters come into view, dwarfed by faces of rock that stand directly across from each other—Mount Hor and Mount Pisgah. Here, cliffs plummet precipitously over 1,000 feet to the glacial waters below. The scenery becomes even more enchanting as you snake your way to the 2,751-foot summit of Pisgah. The trail starts easily on switchbacks. Halfway up, take a slight detour to the left to stand atop Pulpit Rock. This small, semi-circular ledge juts out of Mount Pisgah like a box seat at a Broadway play. The arduous trail proceeds upward in a spiral fashion. On a clear day, you should be able to spot the spine of the Green Mountains and that distinctive peak seen across much of Vermont, Camel's Hump. Who needs to visit nearby St. Johnsbury's Athenaeum and view Albert Bierstadt's famous painting, Domes of Yosemite, when you can see such natural beauty come to life less than an hour north?

3 hours. Moderate. From West Burke, take State Route 5A North for 6 miles to a parking area on the left-hand side, just south of Lake Willoughby. The South Trail begins across the highway.

Mount Mansfield, Stowe, Vermont

Bagging Vermont's highest peak, Mount Mansfield, is a formidable challenge but certainly no strenuous climb like mighty Katahdin. It's a steady ascent that rewards you with views of Lake Champlain in its entirety, Burlington, a 45-minute drive to the East, and the highest peak in New York, Mount Marcy. There are many ways up Mansfield. Families should opt for the Long Trail south from Route 108. A little steeper is the Laura Cowles and Sunset Ridge Trails from the backside at Underhill State Park. Feeling lazy? Drive the toll road or hop in a gondola, which leaves you on the Long Trail, a short distance from the summit. If you really want to test your mettle, go on the Hell Brook trail. The unrelenting path starts from Route 108 at about 1900 feet and 1.3 miles later, you've hit the 4,000-foot mark. It's a favorite of locals as evidenced by the number of Vermonters listed in the logbook at the trailhead. About 2 hours into the climb or the 1.3-mile mark, you'll reach the so-called Adam's Apple of the mountain. There's also the Forehead and Nose of Mansfield, but for some reason The Chin, at 4,393 feet, is the highest point. It must be one of those Yankee chins.

For the Laura Cowles and Sunset Ridge Trails, allow 4-5 hours. From Jeffersonville, take Upper Valley Road toward Underhill Center for approximately 7 miles, until you see a sign for Underhill State Park. Turn left for 3 miles on the dirt road and park in the lot.

Monument Mountain, Great Barrington, Massachusetts

It was August 5, 1850, when writers Nathaniel Hawthorne and Herman Melville met for the first time on a hike up Monument Mountain. Along with Oliver Wendell Holmes, they brought a wagon loaded with picnic food and champagne to keep the conversation lively. Evidently, it rained that day and the literary party took to shelter and drink in a recess on the west side of the mountain. The friendship Hawthorne and Melville developed here would prove to become one of the most significant relationships in American letters. Inspired by his talks with Hawthorne, Melville completed the 600-plus pages of Moby Dick in less than a year. In return, Hawthorne wrote and published another classic work, The House of Seven Gables. The hike up Monument is one of the easiest in the Berkshires, a gradual climb on a well-trodden path through mixed woods of hemlocks, oaks, and beech trees. Less than forty-five minutes later, you're on a summit that Hawthorne said resembled "a headless sphinx wrapped in a Persian shawl." That's one hell of an imagination.

1 1/2 to 2 hours. Easy. The parking lot is located on the left side of Route 7, 3.6 miles north of the Route 23 junction in Great Barrington.

All Aboard, 6 Best Rail-to-Trails

J.P. Morgan, Cornelius Vanderbilt, and the other founding fathers of the Industrial Revolution would be somewhat dismayed if they knew what the majority of their railroad lines were used for today. At the turn of last century, the United States went on the greatest railroad-building spree in history. By 1916, this country had the largest railroad system in the world, with almost 300,000 miles of track. Well, we all know what happened after that. Henry Ford and the Wright Brothers brought about faster, sexier means of transportation that led to eventual decline of the iron horse. Railroad companies went bankrupt and left behind more than 160,000 miles of unused trail. Some rail corridors became roads, but most are vacant, with the dead tracks collecting rust. In the early sixties, however, a small group of locals in southwestern Wisconsin decided to do something creative with their stretch of abandoned railroad. They opened a 32-mile thoroughfare between Elroy and Sparta and designated it a recreational path for bikers and walkers. 60 years later, rail-trails have become a mecca for outdoor enthusiasts and a focal point of urban renewal across the country. Far away from maddening congestion on city streets or the noise of rural highways, these trails offer gentle grades and easy access for outdoor enthusiasts.

Here are six of the best paved bike trails in New England. For the nearest trail to you, visit the **Rail-to-Trails Conservancy**.

Cape Cod Rail Trail, Wellfleet to South Dennis, Massachusetts

The 25-mile Cape Cod Rail Trail lines a corridor that, until 1937, was used to ship cranberries aboard the Old Colony Railroad. Today, the trail is a placid retreat that takes you through the interior of the Cape from Wellfleet to South Dennis, or vice-versa. Starting in Wellfleet, the trail is bordered on both sides by purple wildflowers, flowering dogwood, and small maples, where it's not unusual to find nesting red-winged blackbirds and bright yellow goldfinches. With few hills to tackle, the only obstacles are other runners, rollerbladers, and bikers. The salty air is a pleasant reminder that the Cape Cod National Seashore and its 40-mile stretch of pounding Atlantic surf is never far away. At the Visitors Center in Salt Pond, you can veer off the Cape Cod Rail Trail for 2 miles to lounge on the dunes of Coast Guard Beach. In Orleans, hop off your bikes and snap that quintessential New England shot of fishing boats bobbing in the harbor. Then it's on to the shade of Nickerson Sate Park where you can give your legs a rest and go canoeing on Flax Pond. There's also 13 miles of off-trail riding and hiking hidden in the pitch pine and scrub oak woods. Continue on to Brewster to cool off in a series of swimming holes that are known in these parts as kettle ponds. Seymour, Long and Hinckley ponds are deep freshwater glacial pools with sandy public beaches. Nearby, the now defunct Pleasant Lake General Store in Harwich was once a popular stop on the Old Colony Railroad Line. Cross over Route 6 on Route 124 before veering right through farmland and 100-year-old cranberry bogs, ending in South Dennis.

East Bay Bicycle Path, Providence to Bristol, Rhode Island

All it takes is a mere six miles on a paved path to leave a highly industrialized section of Providence and reach the sheltered coastline of Narragansett Bay. No wonder, locals would rather bike to the beach than deal with car traffic. The 14.5-mile long East Bay Bicycle Path, originally part of the Providence/Worcester line, heads southeast from Providence along the scenic shores of the Bay to the town of Bristol. Less than two miles into the ride, fishing trawlers and sailboats start to appear on the right and small inlets and wetlands can be seen on the left. In the warmer months, you're likely to see locals clamming for littlenecks in the shallow waters along the route. That's quite a contrast from the view of the Providence skyline that lurks behind you. Soon the trail becomes far more suburban as cliffs line the bayside, home to pelicans, egrets, and the occasional swan. South of Riverside, the trail feels more secluded as you head through forest. Prior to mile 6, you reach Haines Park, your first choice of beaches along the route. The trail then swerves inland through the town of Barrington and crosses two wooden bridges before reaching Warren. Just past the 10-mile mark, Warren is the best place to stock up on food and drink. South of Warren, the trail hugs the shoreline of Narragansett once again as the bay widens before reaching the ocean waters. Soon you'll reach Colt State Park and Bristol Town Beach, the finest spot for sunbathing along the route. The trail ends in Bristol at Independence Park, near a handful of seafood restaurant choices that sell freshly caught littleneck clams.

Island Line, Burlington, Vermont

This 14-mile gem of a route hugs the shores of Lake Champlain with the Adirondack Mountains peering down from the New York State side. The Central Vermont Railroad built the line, with the first train arriving in Burlington in December 1849. Within 20 years, Burlington would be the third largest lumber port behind Chicago and Albany. Although the business went into a steady decline leading up to the early 1900s, the railroad continued to thrive through much of the 20th century. Oakledge Park, the starting point on the southeastern side, is one of many spots along the trail where you'll find small beaches and picnic areas. At Roundhouse Point, you'll start to see the first of numerous sailboats tacking across the large lake. North Beach, at the trail's midpoint mark, is a good place to picnic along the rocky shores. One of the best features of the Burlington Bike Path is that you're always a block or two away from a good deli if you need to reenergize.

Norwottuck Rail Trail, Northampton, Massachusetts

Norwottuck, a Native American term for "in the midst of the river," is an appropriate name for this 11-mile bike path that borders the mighty Connecticut River in central Massachusetts. This former Boston & Maine railroad line connected passengers and freight from Northampton to Boston. The last train rolled through in 1980 and the rail trail opened in 1993. One of the highlights is pedaling across the Connecticut River on a 1400-foot long suspension bridge that connects Northampton to Hadley. The route then meanders through open farmland before heading through a tunnel under Route 9. The trail ends at Station Road in South Amherst.

Minuteman Bikeway, Somerville, Massachusetts

Boston's favorite rail-trail, the 10.5-mile Minuteman Bikeway starts in Somerville and swings by a football field, the Alewife MBTA Red Line Station, and the white swans of Spy Pond before connecting with the Arlington portion of the ride. From here, the paved trail follows a former Boston and Maine railroad line behind homes, factories, and warehouses. When you get closer to Lexington, fields of wildflowers and small playgrounds replace the real estate. The trail ends in the small village of Bedford, where you can find ice cream in a former railroad station.

Nashua River Rail Trail, Ayer, Massachusetts to Nashua, New Hampshire

Crossing the New Hampshire border, this 11-mile beauty strip snakes through the towns of Ayer, Groton, Pepperell, and Dunstable, before ending in Nashua. The trail was once part of the Boston & Maine railroad, before stopping freight in 1982. A sylvan slice of New England, snaking through the rolling countryside, the trail is at its best during fall foliage when trees blaze with color.

9 Exceptional
Mountain Biking Locales

There's nothing quite like the exhilarating feeling of mountain biking. The chance to zip down a narrow mountain trail across a shallow stream, to cruise along the banks of a river on a former railroad bed, or to ride on a dirt road through the farmland of Vermont, is a thrill rarely surpassed by any other sport. I never carry a map and I almost always get lost. This might sound foolish to some of you, but not knowing where you are in a New England forest is the equivalent to backpacking in Europe without the slightest care which city you head to next. You create your own route, the reason why I love New England mountain biking. Unlike the West with its 14,000 foot peaks and vast wide-open spaces, New England's parks and forests are compact and far more welcoming. If I take a wrong turn, I don't risk death nor do I spend the night howling with coyotes. Even within the larger state parks mentioned below, you're never more than two to three miles from a dirt road and civilization. These are my favorites, but weave your own web.

The Kingdom Trails, East Burke, Vermont
Just thinking about the Kingdom Trails in autumn, whipping through the red and yellow leaves on the maples behind the Inn at Mountain View Farm, and

I want to jump in my car immediately. This 150-mile circuit, linking former farming roads with slender singletracks, offers the best of Vermont riding. One moment, you're banking narrow turns on Coronary Bypass, the next you're zooming through the tall barren pines in Webs. In fact, it's such a glorious network that you'll want to keep biking even when your legs are cramping and your Camelbak runs dry.

Millstone Hill Touring Center, Barre, Vermont

You might not have heard of Millstone, but once word starts to spread about this unique 70-mile network, expect it to rival the Kingdom Trails as one of the top mountain biking hubs in the state. A century ago, Millstone Hill was home to more than 75 quarry operations. Today, singletracks weave up and down the forest leading to these quarry sites, where you can peer out over the water from atop a large rock pile. Novice riders will also find miles of old quarry roads offering far more moderate biking.

Bartlett Experimental Forest, Bartlett, New Hampshire

One of my favorite spots to ride in the Whites is Bartlett Experimental Forest. Snowmobilers have created a vast network of trails that suit bikers well. The paths climb up and down the mountains and across numerous brooks. Park on Bear Notch Road, just outside Glen, and get ready to cruise on a springy single-track trail that gradually makes its way downhill through the dense blanket of pines and maples, over more than a few streams. It's a spine-tingling run down the mountainside to Route 302. Unfortunately, you now have to make your way back up.

Bear Brook State Park, Allenstown, New Hampshire

You can thank the Seacoast Chapter of the New England Mountain Bike Association for creating and maintaining some of the best trails at Bear Brook. Start with the easy Ferret Trail or the doubletrack, Bobcat. Then move on to the silky smooth Pitch Pine or the root-studded, rock-littered downhill run called Carr Ridge. Bear Hill is a challenging climb, but you'll be rewarded for your efforts with a thrilling downhill. Afterwards, take a bath in Bear Hill Pond to wash off the mud and sweat.

Bradbury Mountain State Park, Pownal, Maine

Your significant other wants to spend the morning shopping in Freeport and you can't stand the thought. Great, drop him off and head ten minutes inland to Pownal, home to Bradbury Mountain. If you want a technical climb to warm you up, start with the O trail.

This leads to other fun trails like Fox East and Ragan. Across the street, near the camping area, there are some relatively new singletracks that will keep you on your toes. The short up and down runs lead to a series of switchbacks, perfect for a good 3-hour spin.

Savoy Mountain State Forest, Florida, Massachusetts

Starting at an elevation over 2,000 feet, Savoy Mountain State Park puts the mountain back into Massachusetts mountain biking. In an area of western Massachusetts known for its abundance of green spaces, the large state forest offers the most extensive network of trails for bikers. Follow the Burnett Pond Trail across New State Road for a sweeping rollercoaster ride through the deep woods. The challenging trail rolls up and down the hillside connecting with Kammick Road to the fire tower atop Border Mountain. This is a good place to relax and take in the vast countryside before biking back down to Burnett Pond.

Arcadia Management Area, Hope Valley, Rhode Island

Situated on the western part of the state, the 13,817-acre Arcadia attracts bikers from as far as Boston and New Haven. Over thirty miles of single-tracks, double-tracks, and dirt roads snake through the forest. Hop on your bike and dip into a shaded thicket of pine, beech, and oak trees. You'll quickly learn that this rural section of Rhode Island near the Connecticut border does indeed have hills. Ride along streams, pass forgotten fishing holes, eventually making your way to the yellow-blazed trail in the far right hand corner of the park that lines Breakheart Pond. Then get lost on a web of trails that branch off like spokes on a wheel. That's the beauty about mountain biking at a place like Arcadia. Unlike road biking, where you always seem to be staring at a map or have that annoying car on your tail, mountain biking offers a liberating feeling of spontaneity. Here, you're free to wander with rarely another biker in sight and the only obstacle, the occasional horseback rider. All the while, smelling the pines and listening to birds.

Pachaug State Forest, Voluntown, Connecticut

Located in the eastern part of the state, Pachaug is Connecticut's largest public space. The 23,000-acre state forest plays host to an incredible amount of single and doubletrack trails. What does that mean to us mountain bikers? A chance to pick a trail, connect the dots, and pedal for as long as our legs can hold up. I usually ride past the H.H. Chapman and Mt. Misery Camping Area signs, turning left at the small Mt. Misery sign. I cruise up and down the small hill, then choose one of the numerous double-tracks that fork off. Make your own loop, have fun, and go early, so you can make it out of this seemingly endless forest by sunset.

Bluff Point Beach, Groton, Connecticut

Mountain biking at the beach might sound like an oxymoron, but at Bluff Point State Park in Groton, a dirt road lines Poquonock River leading straight to the ocean. If you want to ride by your lonesome, numerous singletracks spread out in every direction from the main trail. Choose one and ramble along the shores, or head inland to the John Winthrop house, dating from the early 1700s. Take a breather on the bluffs where you can see directly across the Long Island Sound to New York's Fishers Island and west to Rhode Island's Watch Hill.

Walk this Way, 17 Best Walks

We arrive at the sport where conditioning is unnecessary and your excuses for not doing every one of these walks is unconvincing. All you need is a good pair of walking shoes or sneakers, a bottle of water, perhaps a snack, and a good companion or dog. Enjoy!

Earthplace, the Nature Discovery Center, Westport, Connecticut

Driving past the multi-million dollar estates tucked behind the stone walls of Westport, you finally reach this divine spit of land left undeveloped in suburbia. 62 acres of deciduous forest, open fields, and swamp area border more than two miles of walking trails at **Earthplace**. A good introductory walk is on the Swamp Loop. Birds greet you on the soft trail, a welcome respite from the hum of autos on I-95. Passing through a section of old stately elms, don't be surprised to see wild turkeys wandering the grounds along with deer, pheasants, and the occasional fox.

Harkness Memorial State Park, Waterford, Connecticut

Connecticut's extensive network of Blue-Blazed hiking trails weave across relatively flat terrain, creating one of the best walking systems in the Northeast. The trails are all inland, through forests of maples, oaks, and birches. However, there are several coastal walks not associated with the blue-blazes that are worthy of a visit like the 234-acre Harkness Memorial State Park, a gem in Waterford. Bequeathed to the state in 1952, the 42-room Italianate mansion, manicured lawns and gardens are a perfect place for a stroll or picnic. Tour the house and then head outside on small stony paths that snake through the gardens. In May, this is quite a treat with many of the perennials in bloom. The great expanse of lawn slopes down to the shores. In the summer, a concert series brings well-known performers to the grounds.

Napatree Point, Westerly Rhode Island

For a classic beach walk, try this Long Island Sound stretch of sand that starts near the historic Watch Hill carousel. Listen to the sound of the waves as you saunter along the water on Napatree's crescent-shaped beach. The spit of land curves back towards Rhode Island, similar to the way Provincetown fishhooks on the Cape. As you reach the point, the winds begin to howl, the surf seems a little bit more ominous, and the sand changes to large battered rocks. You can spot the small harbor of Stonington, Connecticut, and the dome of trees atop Fishers Island, New York. On the return trip, view the Victorian houses that cling to the bluffs of Watch Hill.

Cliff Walk, Newport, Rhode Island

Rhode Island's most popular trail is perched on the rocky shores above the Atlantic, ocean on one side, the backyards of the massive Bellevue Avenue mansions on the other. In the summer months, this 3 ½-mile route is crowded with hundreds of folks yearning to see the sloping lawns and backside of those summer "cottages" the Vanderbilts, Whitneys, and Astors built at the turn of the century. Come fall, you'll pass the occasional dog walker as you take in the expanse of the sea all by your lonesome. Park your car on Narragansett Avenue near the walk and proceed to the right. You'll soon spot **The Breakers**, the Italian-style villa commissioned by Cornelius Vanderbilt in 1895. Another highlight is the red and gold lacquered Chinese-style pagoda at the **Marble House**.

World's End, Hingham, Massachusetts

South of Boston, World's End juts out of Hingham Harbor like a rooster at daybreak. In 1890, noted landscape architect Frederick Law Olmstead was hired to transform World's End into a "planned community" of 150 homes. Thankfully, this never came to fruition. The 251-acre estate was farmed and owned by one family until the Trustees of Reservations purchased the property with the help of the public in 1967. A 4-mile walk (jogging is also popular here) starts on a wide path bordered by white pines, hickories, oaks, and bracken ferns. The trail narrows as it hugs the rocky shores of the Atlantic Ocean, with views of the Boston Harbor and the city skyline.

Boston Harbor Islands, Boston, Massachusetts

Quick. Name the group of islands containing the oldest continuously manned lighthouse in the country, a vintage Civil War fort, and the grounds where pirates were hanged in chains as a "spectacle for the warning of others"? Hint: No other area in the United States has so many islands so close to a major city. Yes, they are the Boston Harbor Islands. Take the 45-minute ferry ride from Boston's Long Wharf to Georges Island, where you can visit Fort Warren. Built in 1833, the fort was used in the Civil War as a training ground for Union Troops and prison camp for more than 2,000 Confederate soldiers, including the Vice President of the Confederacy, Alexander Stephens. From Georges, you can board a smaller ferry toward Grape Island. Here, history is replaced by unbridled nature, an ideal spot for walking on grassy paths past fields of wild roses, sumac bushes, pines, towering birches, and thickets of blackberries and raspberries.

Arnold Arboretum, Boston, Massachusetts

It's easy to forget you're still in Boston when walking under century-old elms, maples, and beeches at **Arnold Arboretum**. Located in Jamaica Plain, the 265-acre plot was donated to Harvard University in 1872. The immense botanical garden is known for its exotic array of flora including Australian trees, Japanese Gardens, and every type of rose imaginable, not to mention the hundreds of lilies that bloom around Mother's Day every May. For a great introduction to this wealth of flora, consider taking a 90-minute guided tour offered throughout the year.

Fort Hill Trail, Eastham, Massachusetts

Before you even start the Fort Hill Trail, go across the street and walk under the jaw of a whale, the entrance to Captain Edward Penniman's house.

In the mid-19th century, Penniman climbed the whaling ranks, from harpooner to captain, amassing a fortune in the process. When he returned to the Cape in 1867, he built this house in the ornate Second French Empire Style. Ascend a short hill and you'll be treated to sweeping views of Nauset Marsh and the long stretches of sand at Nauset and Coast Guard Beaches. Heading inland through a section of red cedar trees, the trail arrives at an overlook called Skiff Hill before veering left onto the Red Maple Swamp Trail, my favorite part of the route. A boardwalk snakes over a murky swamp through a copse of tall red maples, evoking the feel of a small enchanted forest.

Broadmoor Wildlife Sanctuary, Natick, Massachusetts

Thankfully, I don't have to travel far to get lost in the woods. Located in the western suburbs, **Broadmoor** is a 600-acre sanctuary run by the Massachusetts Audubon Society. Nine miles of trails weave over marsh and the Charles River on boardwalks and into a thick forest of tall pines. Rest atop one of the bridges to look for great blue herons as they spread their wings and take flight. Or picnic on a bench near a small waterfall. Other birds include kingfishers, osprey, and wood ducks.

Walden Pond, Concord, Massachusetts

"I went to the woods because I wished to live deliberately, to front only the essential facts of life, and see if I could not learn what it had to teach, and not, when I came to die, discover that I had not lived," wrote Henry David Thoreau in his best known work, Walden. Thoreau ventured to the woods with ax in tow in March 1845, to build his historic hut. Never would this modest writer imagine what an impact his philosophical musings would have on the world 165 years later. For two years, two months, and two days, Thoreau lived alone in the woods, a mile from any neighbor, in his rustic abode built near the shores of Walden Pond in Concord. While a replica of the hut only exists now, the woods make for a wonderful ramble, especially in the early morning hours.

Fox Research and Demonstration Forest, Hillsborough, New Hampshire

In 1922, Caroline Fox bequeathed to the state of New Hampshire her 348-acre farm with house and barn. The state has since added more land, totaling 1445 acres, built an environmental center, forestry museum, and created more than 20 miles of well-marked trails through the woods. Indeed, most of the abandoned farmland Ms. Fox left to the state is now woods, perfect for strolling. This includes the 4.5-mile Ridge Trail, which winds through a forest of maples, pines, hemlocks, and birch before arriving at Mud Pond.

Sabbaday Falls, Waterville Valley, New Hampshire

Families with young children will appreciate this easy walk off the Kancamagus Highway, 16 miles west of Concord and the junction of Route 112. The one-mile round-trip jaunt winds through tall birches and beeches before heading down the stone steps to Sabbaday Falls. Watch the cascading waters plummet over the rocks into a pool of water, just dessert for toddlers and their parents who made the trek.

Marsh-Billings-Rockefeller National Historic Park, Woodstock, Vermont

When I think of an idyllic late autumn stroll, crunching over fallen leaves on a deeply forested trail while breathing in the first chill of winter, this is the place that comes to mind. **Marsh-Billings-Rockefeller** is the first unit of the National Park System to focus on the theme of conservation history and stewardship, the main concern of Frederick Billings. Beginning in the 1870s, Billings designed a forest with numerous tree plantations and constructed a 20-mile network of carriage roads to showcase his work. Tour the exhibits in the Carriage Barn, then hit the carriage path trails through Billings' dream 550-acre forest. 11 of Billings' original plantings remain including groves of Norwegian spruce and Scottish Pine from the 1880s, mixed in with an indigenous Vermont blend of white pine and white ash. The longest carriage path trail circles around The Pogue, a gem of water backed by Mount Tom.

West River Trail, Jamaica State Park, Jamaica, Vermont

This riverbank trail, located along the West River in Jamaica State Park, follows an old railroad bed that was built in 1881 and long ago lapsed into decay. The highlight is Hamilton Falls, which tumbles and pools spectacularly down 125 feet of granite ledges, making it Vermont's highest waterfall. If there's a fall dam release from the Ball Mountain Dam upriver, you'll get to see whitewater paddlers tackle The Dumplings, a set of enormous boulders.

The Marginal Way, Ogunquit, Maine

Newport's Cliff Walk boasts exquisite ocean views and a close-up peek of the Gatsbyesque mansions. Prouts Neck's rocky shoreline will always be known as the place where a painter named Winslow Homer woke up early to take his daily stroll with his dog, Sam. Unfortunately, neither of those walks leave you at **Barnacle Billy's**, a beloved lobster-in-the-rough joint in Perkins Cove. Ogunquit's Marginal Way rises atop the rugged shoreline, rewarding folks with views of pocket-sized beaches buttressed by boulders as you amble by century-old cedar trees and pines that have been stunted by the wind. The paved trail is accessible to all, from babies in strollers to the elderly in wheelchairs. Once in Perkins Cove, order that cup of chowder and lobster roll at the counter and grab a seat on the deck overlooking the harbor while you wait for your number to be called. You can simply make the return trip on the Marginal Way or take a trolley back into town.

Cliff Walk, Prouts Neck, Maine

The small town of Prouts Neck has changed little since Winslow Homer painted every nook and cranny of these shores from 1883 to 1910. Outside **Homer's studio**, juniper trees, planted by Homer, slope down from his backyard to the moors, eventually reaching the jagged Maine gray rock that lines most of the Neck's shore. The best way to celebrate Homer is to follow in his footsteps and take the same walk Homer took many mornings with his dog, Sam, a white wire-haired terrier. The mile-long Cliff Walk created by Winslow's brother, Charles, was designed to preserve the most scenic part of the peninsula. Even to this day, the Prouts Neck Association has kept this boulder-strewn shoreline free of all houses so walkers have an unfettered view of those crashing waves. An added bonus is the chance to tour Homer's former studio with the Portland Museum of Art.

Rockland Breakwater, Rockland, Maine

If you want to feel like you're at the edge of the world, take this enjoyable stroll to the Rockland lighthouse on the longest rock jetty in New England. The walk is a visual feast at sunset, when the last rays of the day filter down to the large rock slabs and seals can often be found resting ashore. To your right, Rockland's historic schooners are docked in the harbor. To your left, the mountains of Camden Hills State Park stand watch over Maine's rugged coastline. Jeeps were once permitted on the stone jetty, resulting in large cracks, so be careful. Walk to the end of the breakwater on the far side of the lighthouse to view the last round of boats and ferries gliding into the harbor. Then make the round-trip back to your car, which can be parked on streets on the perimeter of the Samoset Resort.

New England's Best Botanical Garden

Coastal Maine Botanical Garden, Boothbay Harbor, Maine

One of the hidden gems along the mid-Maine coast is the **Coastal Maine Botanical Gardens**. Stroll through the Butterfly House to see the intriguing caterpillars (one looked like an Australian aboriginal art painting) and butterflies. Then wander around the Garden of the Five Senses, a real highlight. Smell the sweet lemon verbena, touch the soft, velvety lamb's ear, and take off your shoes to walk on the smooth stones of the reflexology spiral. Just as magical is the Children's Garden, where the stone paths lead to fish-filled ponds, oversized cabbages, hungry chickens, and small huts filled with hand-made puppet-sized fairies. Adults seem to have just as much fun as the children. In spring and summer, flowers always seem to be in bloom, like the rows of white hydrangea and sweet-smelling roses we had the pleasure to see when we were last there.

8 Trustees of Reservations Sites Not To Be Overlooked

In 1891, Boston landscape architect Charles Eliot received the go-ahead from the state legislature to establish **The Trustees of Reservations** "for the purposes of acquiring, holding, maintaining and opening to the public...beautiful and historic places... within the Commonwealth." Today, the non-profit conservation organization maintains 118 sites in Massachusetts and has a yearly membership over 100,000 people. Crane Beach is the crown jewel in the TTOR collection. Others, like these eight locales are less heralded, but just as worthy for an outing:

Long Hill, Beverly, Massachusetts

As editor and publisher of the Atlantic Monthly, Ellery Sedgwick worked with some of the finest writers of his time, including Ernest Hemingway and Robert Frost. Yet, it's his marriages to not one, but two accomplished gardeners and horticulturists that has had far more of a lasting impression. In 1916, Sedgwick moved with his first wife, Mabel, to a 114-acre hillside property in the North Shore. The house sits atop a drumlin staring out at forest, but it's the wonderful gardens at Long Hill that will capture your attention. No matter what season you visit, there will be something in bloom, from blue forget-me-nots to exotic Chinese redbuds to the soft yellow and very rare Molly the Witch peonies. The assemblage of trees is also intriguing, from the tall dawn redwood planted by Sedgwick's second wife, Marjorie, to the signature copper beech in front of the house close to a century old.

Westport Town Farm, Westport, Massachusetts
Heading to Westport Town Farm on a bucolic stretch of road, you'll no doubt pass kayakers and stand-up paddleboarders cruising down the Westport River. The wooden clapboard 1824 house at Westport Town Farm is a welcome introduction to this pastoral property perched on a hill overlooking the river. Still a working farm, the Trustees donate produce to area hunger relief agencies and hold a weekly Farmers Market on Saturdays in summer. Take the grassy trail past the barnyard onto pasture that slopes down to the water's edge. You'll be accompanied by birdsong.

Mytoi and Cape Poge Wildlife Refuge, Martha's Vineyard, Massachusetts
Beach lovers headed to East Beach on Chappaquiddick have to pass the Japanese-style garden called Mytoi. Worthy of a stop, azaleas, daffodils, dogwoods, and rhododendrons line the freshwater creeks. The dirt road eventually crosses a bridge, stopping at East Beach. Walk the beach to see one of the most pristine stretches of coastline on the Atlantic. Part of the Cape Poge Wildlife Refuge, this barrier beach is the best place to birdwatch on the Vineyard. Ospreys, oystercatchers, piping plovers, terns, and the occasional bald eagle nest here. To get a close up look at

the birds, sign up for the guided kayak tour with the Trustees.

Tully Lake Campground, Royalston, Massachusetts

Come to this tranquil lake where there is little or no motorized boat traffic and tents-only campsites and you'll understand why campers return year after year. Many bring their own kayaks to paddle to the sandy isles along the sinuous Tully River. The Trustees offers kayak rentals and stand-up paddleboarding lessons on Sundays in season. Hiking trails lead to scenic Doane's Falls, where Lawrence Brook tumbles over a series of ledges before it reaches Tully Lake. Rangers leads paddlers to see beavers and teach kids how to fish. You may want to bring your mountain bike, since there's a 7-mile loop around Long Pond.

Chesterfield Gorge, Chesterfield, Massachusetts

The sound of rushing water serves as a welcome mat to Chesterfield Gorge. Here, the East Branch of the Westfield River drops dramatically through rock walls that are close to 70-feet high. Below the gorge, fly-fishermen are usually seen casting their lines in the riffles in hopes of hooking a trout. Take deep breaths of sweet pine as you walk through the thick forest on the East Branch Trail. This 7-mile long dirt road is open to both hikers and mountain bikers who can ride through neighboring Gilbert Bliss State Forest.

William Cullen Bryant Homestead, Cummington, Massachusetts

Stroll under the ancient-looking sugar maples and hemlocks William Cullen Bryant's family planted 200 years ago, when the great poet was just a boy, and you'll reach a rivulet. The Trustees has posted Bryant's entire poem from 1823, "The Rivulet," next to the stream. "The same sweet sounds are in my ear, my early childhood loved to hear," wrote Bryant. Long after his family had sold off the land and moved to Illinois to farm, the poet and abolitionist would buy the land back in 1865, the same year his good friend Abraham Lincoln was assassinated. Bryant, as he documents so well in his poetry, always preferred country life to city life and he would spend all of his summers here until his death in 1878. Look out at the meadows, forest, and Berkshire foothills and you realize little has changed thanks to conservation efforts. It's still a slice of sylvan heaven, one that's best observed with a picnic lunch made by the Old Creamery, just down the road.

Naumkeag, Stockbridge, Massachusetts

Formerly owned by the Choate Family of New York before it was bequeathed to The Trustees of Reservations in 1958, Naumkeag is a 44-room Berkshires "Cottage" from the Gilded Age, filled with arts, antiques, and collections around from around the world. But it's the outdoor gardens that truly inspire, a masterpiece of 30 years of collaborative work by former owner, Mabel Choate, and her dear friend, Fletcher Steele, one of America's first modern landscape architects. Described by the Library of American Landscape History as a "playground for the imagination," The Trustees have just completed a 3-year, $3 million garden and landscape restoration project designed to rejuvenate the gardens and bring them back to Choate and Steele's original vision. The transformation includes the renovation of Fletcher Steele's iconic Blue Steps, one of the most photographed features in 20th-century American landscape design.

Bartholomew's Cobble, Sheffield, Massachusetts

At the southernmost point of the Berkshires, near the Connecticut border, you'll find Bartholomew's Cobble. Walking on the Ledges Trail, the Housatonic River snakes through dairy farms on the left while eroding limestone and quartzite rocks form the cobble to your right. Take a slight detour at Corbin's Neck to get a closer view of the river and the cows resting on its banks. Then continue on the Tulip Tree Trail to stroll uphill through a forest of tall hemlocks before reaching a clearing. At a short summit, take advantage of the bench to sit and take in the views of Mount Everett and Mount Race, part of the Appalachian Trail.

10 Ways to Enjoy Acadia National Park

While other national parks wow you with their impressive towering peaks or voluminous canyons, **Acadia National Park** in coastal Maine is best known for its boulder-strewn coastline, short summits overlooking the ocean, and a network of former carriage path trails that weave through the deep forest of pines and birches. This breathtaking coastal scenery, located primarily on Mount Desert Island, was thankfully preserved and is now one of America's oldest national parks. Yet, it's not just the serene locale, the lobster dinners, and the salty air that lures families again and again to this remote retreat. No, it's the taste of the wilderness that's easily accessible for all ages.

Bike the Carriage Path Trails

Off limits to motorized vehicles, these wide hard packed gravel trails lead bikers to some of the most secluded parts of Acadia National Park. The 43-mile network is ideal for inexperienced mountain bikers. Start by circling the shores of Eagle Lake, Acadia's second largest body of water. Under a forest of spruce, you steadily climb counterclockwise, only to coast downhill when Cadillac Mountain dramatically comes into view. Far more remote is The Amphitheater Loop, used primarily by local dog walkers. Park your car at the Brown Mountain

Gate House off Route 198 and begin to pedal uphill, quickly getting glimpses of the ever-present Atlantic. The 4.4-mile loop becomes a magical up and down run through dense woods. A highlight is the chance to ride across the Amphitheater Bridge, the longest of John D. Rockefeller's original overpasses.

Sea Kayak Frenchman Bay

During the summer months, the Park Loop can be as crowded as 5th Avenue in midtown Manhattan. That's why one of the finest ways to see Acadia National Park during high peak season is from a distance, with your head and feet only inches away from the water line. Sea kayaking around the phalanx of small islands that line Frenchman Bay is the perfect escape from the traffic jams in Bar Harbor. **Coastal Kayaking** offers daily 4-hour guided tours of the waters surrounding Acadia. They'll fit you for life jackets, sea skirts, and booties and off you go with van and kayaks to the bar of Bar Harbor, a sand spit that juts out of town at low tide. You'll paddle around the northern shores of Bar Island, where bright pink starfish lie on the rocks, and then continue around Sheep Porcupine Island, where porpoises and seals are often found playing. Guides usually stop for a 15-minute break at The Hop, a small island at the northernmost tip of Long Porcupine Island, so everyone can stretch their legs before making the return trip.

Hike Acadia Mountain

A mere 681 feet high, the short peak of Acadia Mountain overlooks much of Acadia National Park.

The trail is situated on the island's far less congested western side, where you'll rarely see more than a handful of climbers even in mid-summer. The path curves slowly through copses of birches before crossing an abandoned road and heading up. Before you can swat that incredibly annoying black fly, you're the next Sir Edmund Hillary. From atop your perch, the Cranberry Islands look like peas in a pod, and numerous yachts are safely anchored in Southwest Harbor. Yet, that view pales in comparison to Norumbega Mountain, which slopes sharply into Somes Sound creating the only fjord in New England.

1 to 2 hours. Easy. The trailhead is located 3 miles south of Somesville on Route 102. Park at the small lot where the Acadia Mountain sign is clearly hung. The path is located across Route 102.

Sail a Friendship Sloop

If you truly want to feel like a local on Mount Desert Island, take a day sail on a Friendship Sloop from Northeast or Southwest Harbor. **Sail Acadia** offers the opportunity to take a 3-hour guided sail on three Friendship Sloops, vessels that were used during the late 1800s to fish for lobsters along the Frenchman Bay shoreline. We sailed on the Helen Brooks, past the estates lining the Northeast Harbor shores. Soon we were gliding at a good 5-knot clip towards Great Cranberry Island and the many lobstermen picking up their traps. With a 6-foot keel, these sailboats can weather the strong gusts and fog often found along the Maine coast. Edged with spruce wood, the Helen Brooks is also a stylish ride. Near the beach at Manset, we spotted two porpoises gracefully arching their backs in and out of the choppy water. Then we sailed past Southwest Harbor into Somes Sound, Acadia Mountain to the left and Norumbega Mountain to the right, standing tall as gatekeepers to this long inlet. The mix of mountains, offshore islands, and granite-lined shoreline could easily entice the most jaded sailor to buy his own sloop and sail these legendary cruising grounds on a daily basis. Far too quickly, we were back on the docks of Northeast Harbor.

Bike Schoodic Peninsula

If they call the western half of Mount Desert Island the Quiet Side, they should call Schoodic Peninsula the Secret Side. Still part of Acadia National Park, Schoodic is a good hour's drive from Bar Harbor, so few people outside of Mainers in the know head here. Do yourself a favor and follow their cue. You'll thank me. On a day when two large cruise ships dropped off over 4,000 people into Bar Harbor, we took a ferry smaller than a tugboat, The Quoddy Bay, to Winter Harbor, the gateway to the Schoodic Peninsula. There's no longer any need to drive to Schoodic, especially if you want to bike the 10 to 12-mile loop. You can get here on a scenic hour-long boat ride, mesmerized by the views of pine-studded islands, the mountainous shoreline, and the granite cliffs. The paved Park Loop is one way with two lanes, so cars can easily pass you. They recently created 8 miles of carriage path trails, hard-packed gravel routes only available to bikers and hikers. After taking the Park Loop, return via the carriage path trails, crossing the entirety of the peninsula and past a national park campground. Bike along the rocky shoreline and stop to walk atop a breakwater and watch the tide rush out to sea. All around you is the Atlantic with another memorable seascape to savor, be it a lone sailboat gliding through the open water, an unchartered island just offshore, or pink granite ledges that form one of the highlights, Schoodic Point.

Rock Climb Otter Cliffs

Superior rock climbing may be Acadia's best-kept secret. The same glacially carved granite cliffs and faces that challenge experts are also available to novices. The two most popular areas are Otter Cliffs, a 60-foot sea cliff, and the south wall of Mount Champlain, 200 feet high, set in from the ocean but with incredible views. **Atlantic Climbing** takes beginners on half-day classes to Otter Cliffs, a top-roping area with great climbs like Wonderwall (5.6). It is also home to the epic A Dare By the Sea (5.10+). Among the less crowded areas, Atlantic Climbing recommends South Bubble and Great Head, another sea cliff.

Hop Aboard Diver Ed

During the winter, former harbor master Eddie Monat dives for scallops. For close to 20 years in the summer months, he's been leading trips out on the bay to find the creatures lurking in the deep. He's not just a College of the Atlantic-educated naturalist, but a highly entertaining performer who has everyone on the boat laughing hysterically, whether your children are aged 4, 14, or 44. Equipped with a high-def video camcorder, **Diver Ed** swims along the floor of the sea, finding sea cucumbers, rock crabs, sand dollars, and starfish. You watch his every move on a large movie screen on deck, narrated by his wife, Captain Evil. He brings along his version of Mr. Bill, "Mini Ed," who unfortunately gets the bulk of the lobster's wrath, his head clawed repeatedly. When Diver Ed returns to the boat, he brings along his bag of booty that everyone gets to touch in the large tank.

Walk the Ocean Path

Unless you're a hardcore hiker, forego the steep Precipice Trail, where steel rungs lead climbers on a ladder up the sheer cliff walls. Instead, park at Sand Beach on the Park Loop and walk along the Ocean Path, an apt name for the trail that laces the rocky shoreline. Stop at Thunder Hole, where on days where the waves crash against the bedrock you can hear a deafening boom close to a quarter mile away. Then walk along the boulder-strewn coastline to Otter Point, at the end of the peninsula. Gazing at the terraced stone that lines the water and the bend of the island as it reaches the tall pines of Otter Point, you immediately realize why this patch of stunning scenery is preserved forever as the Northeast's lone national park.

Popovers at Jordan Pond Gatehouse

Lunch at Jordan Pond Gatehouse is a rite of passage in these parts. Grab one of the picnic tables on the sloping manicured lawn and revel in the view of South Bubble and Penobscot Mountain looming over the pond waters. Then dig into the hot-out-of-the-oven homemade popovers, bowls of seafood chowder, and cranberry salad topped with curried chicken, all washed down with strawberry lemonade. The highlight for all will be another popover, this one dripping wet in hot chocolate sauce and topped with a scoop of mocha ice cream.

Lobster Rolls at Beal's or Thurston's

For the requisite lobster roll and clam chowder, grab a picnic table at **Beal's** overlooking the lobstermen in the small fishing village of Southwest Harbor. Toddler-friendly fare includes chicken nuggets, fish and chips, and grilled cheese sandwiches. **Thurston's** rivals Beal's as another class lobster-in-the rough joint.

5 Great Fall Foliage Activities Away from the Crowds

Leave the car behind and immerse yourselves in nature to best appreciate the foliage splendor. Hike, bike, paddle, or stroll on any of these routes and, more than likely, you'll leave the crowds behind as well:

Canoe the Allagash River, Maine

92 miles long, the Allagash Wilderness Waterway slips off the map of America, remote and isolated, hundreds of miles from the nearest metropolis. Early autumn is the time of year when the usual mute moose is as talkative as Bullwinkle (two moose in heat almost trampled over my tent one memorable night), the leaves on the hillside are aflame with fall foliage color, and there are few other humans on the river. Canoeing the entire Allagash takes from 7 to 10 days to complete, but you can take it in chunks. Many paddlers put-in at Chamberlain Lake and take out near the village of Allagash. If you want to go with a guided group, Registered Maine Guides Lani Love and Chip Cochrane of **Allagash Canoe Trips** have been guiding paddlers down the Allagash for more than 30 years.

Hike the Bubbles, Acadia National Park

Flooded with tourists in July and August, the country's national parks are far less frequented in the fall, almost returning to their original wild state. This is especially true of Acadia in autumn, when thickets of maples on Mt. Desert Island turn a shade crimson to add to the already spectacular light show of dark blue ocean and evergreen forest. An added bonus is that black flies and mosquitoes are a distant memory. Head to the Bubbles, just off the Park Loop, to find pockets of maples on the hillside. A rocky staircase at North Bubble leads through a leaf-strewn path to a flat boulder atop the summit, the perfect vantage point to view Jordan Pond to the south. Afterwards, reward yourself with lunch at nearby Jordan Pond Gatehouse.

Hike to Champney Falls off the Kancamagus Highway, New Hampshire

Champney Falls Trail is one of the few trails in America to be named after an artist, in this case, Benjamin Champney, whose paintings of Mount Chocorua in the 1850s can be found in Boston's Museum of Fine Arts. The distinctive silhouette of Mount Chocorua was favored by landscape artists not only for its grandeur, but also for its association with the 18th-century legend of its namesake, a Native American chief who died on the slopes. Starting at the trailhead, just off that beloved fall foliage route, the Kancamagus Highway, the path meanders along a rushing brook. Hop on rocks across a stream and follow the soft root-littered trail gradually uphill. You'll soon reach majestic Champney Falls and the glorious rush of water as it cascades down a series of ledges into rivulets and pools. Beyond Champney Falls is the aptly named Pitcher Falls, where water flows from a much higher altitude as if being poured from a pitcher. The falls can be reached in an hour from the trailhead. If you came to bag the distinctive 3,490-foot summit of Chocorua, your day has just begun.

Golf the Equinox Course, Manchester, Vermont

When Louise Orvis and the other women of southern Vermont were denied membership to neighboring Ekwanok Country Club in 1927, she hired Walter Travis to carve a course out of the valley at the base of Mt. Equinox. Now part of the **Equinox Resort**, the design was updated by Rees Jones and what a beauty it is. Climbing through the pine, birch, and maples, you're surrounded by mountains. Now managed by Troon, the course reads short but plays long, opening with a nice par-4 downhill to get golfers warmed up. Soon you're attempting the seventh, the memorable "road hole," a long par-five that plays over a public road. Stop for lunch at the Dormy Grill, overlooking the ninth green and order the signature lobster roll. If you were wise, you spent the night prior at the iconic resort so you can snag a coveted early morning tee time.

Horseback Ride at Vermont Icelandic Horse Farm, Waitsfield, Vermont

In a state known for the imposing Morgan horse, the small pony-sized Icelandic horse is a special treat. Icelandics move at a very steady pace without much rocking, like driving a car with good shock absorbers. Based in in the town of Fayston, three miles off Route 100 in the northern end of Waitsfield,

Icelandic Horse Farm offers hourly to half-day to full-day rides. A typical full day ride will take you, on average, 15 miles, through the foliage-saturated woods of Mad River Valley and on country roads.

5 Special Spots to Bird Watch

Back home in suburban Boston, I keep a pair of binoculars handy near my desk. I never thought of myself as a bird watcher, just someone with a couple bird feeders in the backyard, hoping to spot that fleeting yellow warbler in the spring and the beady-eyed red tailed hawk in late fall. I can certainly understand the allure of finding new birds in the wild, watching a great blue heron take flight on a serpentine river, spotting a ruby-throated hummingbird feed in the bushes, or staring in awe at the regal eagle, yet I'm not quite ready to start compiling a list. Thankfully, New England doesn't discriminate based on expertise. A dote like me can have just as much fun bird-watching during all four seasons as the most avid lister. There are some 300 species of birdlife in the region, from the everyday blue jay to wild turkeys to endangered piping plovers nesting on the shores of Nantucket and Martha's Vineyard. Then there are the special finds that might take a little more effort to seek out, but memorable once you arrive:

Connecticut Audubon Coastal Center, Milford Point, Connecticut

Migrating shorebirds are prevalent along the Connecticut shoreline in late spring and fall. Green backed herons, yellow warblers, snowy egrets, swallows, ospreys, doves, and Canadian geese are just some of the birds sighted along the tidal pools and beaches of the coast. The 840-acre **Connecticut Audubon Coastal Center** at Milford Point is one of the best spots in the state for birding. Of the 399 species known in Connecticut, over 300 have been recorded here. There are nesting piping plovers, least terns, American oystercatchers (rare in state), and both types of night herons. Ask about their naturalist-guided canoe trips to the Charles E. Wheeler State Wildlife Management Area, one of the few remaining unaltered areas on the Connecticut coast.

Plum Island, Newburyport, Massachusetts

The finest birdwatching along the Massachusetts coast occurs at the Parker River National Wildlife Refuge on Plum Island. The northern third of this eight-mile long barrier island (30 miles north of Boston) is developed, with the remainder containing this 4,662-acre refuge. Wander through the barrier beach, thickets, and salt marshes to view up to 350 species of feathered friends. Beaches on the refuge are closed during the prime sunning months of June, July, and August, so that the short, stocky endangered piping plovers can nest undisturbed. Although the beach is off limits, the marsh is still an excellent area to spot migrating shore birds like black-bellied plovers, short-billed dowitchers, and sandpipers. The boardwalk on the Hellcat Swamp Trail circles around the murky grasses to an observation tower and blind. Park at Parking Lot #4 to start the trail. At the salt pans, spend time scanning for hawks, egrets, and herons. Avoid early to mid-July when biting Greenhead flies are on the rampage.

Wellfleet Bay Wildlife Sanctuary, Wellfleet, Massachusetts

While the interior of Cape Cod is rich with cardinals, mockingbirds, goldfinches and woodpeckers, it's the coastal variety that entice many a visitor here. Shorebirds by the thousands, returning from their Arctic breeding grounds, stop along the Cape coast for much needed respite and food as they fatten up for their journey south. One of their favorite overnights is **Wellfleet Bay Wildlife Sanctuary**. The Massachusetts Audubon Society, who own and maintain the property, have claimed to have seen over 250 different species like oystercatchers, stilts, avocets, plovers, turnstones, and sandpipers. The Goose Pond Trail is a leisurely ramble though marsh, forest, ponds, and fields. At low tide, continue on the Try Island Trail to a boardwalk that leads to Cape Cod Bay. Green herons and large goose-like brants are prevalent in the surrounding salty marsh. Retrace your steps back to the Goose Pond Trail to reach Goose Pond. A bench overlooking the water is one of the most serene spots on the Cape. Northern hummingbirds fly in and out of the branches overhead forming a choir whose voices will soothe any man's soul.

Odiorne Point State Park, Portsmouth, New Hampshire

The only spit of undeveloped coastline in the state, Odiorne Point is situated on the far end of Portsmouth Harbor. 135 acres of protected land make this a routine stop for our feathered friends along the Atlantic Flyway. It's a good place to find black-backed gulls feeding along the shores or watch for double-crested cormorants drying their wings on the rocks. A 2-mile loop along the coast is a favorite of birdwatchers.

Machias Seal Island, Off of Cutler, Maine

Near the mouth of the Bay of Fundy, Machias Seal Island is a tiny unspoiled sanctuary for a number of Maine's most noted marine bird species. You can visit the island via a charter boat operating out of Cutler for the nine-mile cruise out to sea. An hour later you disembark onto a small low-lying island. Hundreds of plump birds whiz over your heads searching the waters for breakfast. Some have hooded black heads that look like Batman's disguise. These are the razorbill auks. Others have eyes the size of a parrot with beaks dotted red, black, and yellow. This is the bird everyone is excited to see, the Atlantic puffin. Weather permitting, you can climb atop the seaweed-slick rocks and see puffins two to three feet away. The eastern part of the island is covered with Arctic terns. The razorbill auks might look like superheroes, but it is the aggressive tern that keeps predators like seagulls away from the eggs of all the island's birds. Paths lead to four blinds where you can set up shop and watch the puffins return to feed their young. The **Barbara Frost** leaves daily from late May to mid-August. Book 2022 cruises as soon as the trips open up in early January 2021. Cost is $160 per person for the five-hour outing.

4 Places to Sea Kayak

Shrouded in an early morning mist, the fog recedes and we are treated to a view of Maine's coastline few ever see. The battering surf of the Northern Atlantic thrusts against a boulder-strewn coastline, spewing foam high into the air. Juniper pines, dwarfed by forceful gales, refuse to budge from the land above. Safely protected in my shell of a kayak, I hold onto a lobster buoy, not wanting to be sucked into the middle of the ocean's reunion with land. I veer toward the open water, following my group of propeller-style paddlers. It's day three of a six-day inn-to-inn sea kayaking tour of Maine's mid-coast organized by outfitter, Mountain Travel Sobek. While daily sightings of cormorants, ospreys, and seals are common, Homo sapiens are rarely seen or heard until we venture out of our boats in the late afternoon to shower and dine at sumptuous inns. All it takes is one morning or afternoon out paddling in the ocean waters to understand the allure of this sport. Sample these 4 spots as starters:

Thimble Islands, Branford, Connecticut
Southeast of Branford, the small picturesque fishing harbor of Stony Creek is the gateway to a group of 32 inhabited islands known as the Thimble Islands. An apt name, some of these islands are just large enough to hold one house, as if the islands were nothing

more than houseboats at their moorings. Others have longs stretches of untrammeled beach, ideal for small boat travel. **Branford River Paddlesports** features guided half-day, sunset, even full moon paddles around the Thimbles. Expect to hear the lore about Captain Kidd's hidden treasure on Money Island (no one's ever found it) and General Tom Thumb's courtship of a diminutive gal on Cut-in-Two Island. P.T. Barnum broke it off and had Tom marry another one of his circus's little people. Bare Island was once a granite quarry. Indeed, Stony Creek granite can be found in such famous structures as the Lincoln Memorial and the Brooklyn Bridge. Come have a look at a leisurely pace.

Essex River Basin, Essex, Massachusetts

The web of estuaries in Essex Marsh, an hour north of Boston in Cape Ann, leads to protected bays and the backside of Crane Beach. These tidal flats are home to thousands of littleneck clams, your entrée of choice at nearby Woodman's seafood restaurant after a day of paddling.

Essex River Basin Adventures offers three to five-hour tours from the estuaries of the Essex River to Hog Island.

Peaks Island, Maine

While lobsterman ply the ocean waters for their catch, Portland executives play in the ocean with their shiny new kayaks. Follow their lead into the open water to paddle around a handful of the 220 Casco Bay Islands (only a quarter of them are inhabited).

Casco Bay Lines leaves every hour in the summer for the 20-minute cruise to Peaks Island. Once there, you can hook up with **Maine Island Kayak Company** for full-day and half-day paddles. On the half-day paddle, you'll slide into your kayaks and paddle over to Fort Gorges, built just before the Civil War in 1858. Atop the thick stone walls of the Fort, you can see the Portland waterfront in all its rugged grandeur. Huge cranes fix the larger boats of the cruise fleet while oil storage tanks dot the wharves. As you make your way around the northern tip of Great Diamond Island, be on the lookout for ospreys nesting in the tall pines that line the granite shores. Further inland, houses are being built to accommodate more year-round commuters who yearn to have the sea as their welcome mat. After this little jaunt, you might make that same move.

Sheepscot Bay, Georgetown, Maine

North of Freeport, fingers of land dangle down from coastal Route 1 to create miles of sheltered bays to paddle. One of my favorite spots is Georgetown, where I usually rent a room from **Coveside B&B** and have **Seaspray Kayaking** out of Brunswick deliver an oceanworthy kayak to their docks. Careful not to start or end near low tide (or I'll be digging for clams in the muck), I paddle south past the lobster boats to the **Five Islands Lobster Company** wharf. On the way, I spot ospreys sitting atop their over-sized nests, seals, and the distinctive orange beak of the American Oystercatcher. Yet, it's paddling north on Little Sheepscot River, sheltered from the surf by MacMahan Island, that I truly cherish. The boulder-strewn shoreline is draped in seaweed and topped with velvety moss, creating a soothing, shady retreat in the late afternoon hours.

5 Places to Canoe or Kayak

Whether you like to put in on the quiet water of a backwoods pond, run a leisurely float-and-paddle down a mild quickwater river, or go on overnights on the long sinuous rivers of Maine, the Northeast is one of the premier canoeing destinations in the country. Tensions turn to tranquility on waters where loons replace the loonies of the city. Here's some ideas to get you started:

The Maine Waterways with Mahoosuc Guide Service

Many of the old-time Maine guides have retired or perished in the past decade, leaving behind a historic legacy of paddlers who know the Maine Woods waterways like the lines on the back of their hands. Thankfully, Kevin Slater of **Mahoosuc Guide Service** is still working and leading affordable camping adventures through the Maine interior on legendary rivers like the Allagash or Penobscot. The 17-foot long wood and canvas canoes you'll sit in are all created by Slater. It takes him more than 120 hours of work to carve one of these delicately ribbed beauties out of northern white cedar and cherry wood, using only native varieties. His skilled craftsmanship was passed down from his mentor, a Wabanaki Indian. Travel with Slater on a 5-day jaunt in this maze of blue waterways, a seemingly countless number of lakes, rivers, streams, and ponds that branch off in every direction to form this capillary system deep in the forest, and you'll soon forget all about the woes of modernity. In its place will be daily sightings of moose, beaver, maybe even bear as you stop to fish for salmon.

Umbagog Lake, Errol, New Hampshire

At the junction of Routes 16 and 26 in Errol, **Northern Waters Outfitters** rents canoes. By all means, grab one and put-in north of town on Route 16 to find out why Umbagog Lake was named a National Wildlife Refuge. A short paddle on the Androscoggin River, which empties into Umbagog, brings you to a deserted island where atop one dead pine tree is a large nest. Every year since 1988, a family of bald eagles has called this nest home, giving birth in springtime to their young. The eagles arrive in early spring and stay until the Androscoggin freezes over in early January. We've been to Umbagog three times, usually in August when the white heads of the parents guard the nest as their children learn to fly. Loons, Canada geese, and herons lounge in the water of this quiet lake on the Maine border, yet it's the pair of nesting bald eagles that headline this day's activity.

Saco River, Conway, New Hampshire

When your legs are weary from days of arduous hiking in the Whites, let your arms take over and canoe down the Saco River. The narrow waterway weaves from Crawford Notch in the heart of the White Mountains all the way through southeastern Maine, before emptying into the Atlantic at the city of Saco, south of

Portland. In Conway, there are any number of access points and canoeing options along the Saco, from a 3-mile trip to a three-day, 40-mile canoe-camping journey to Hiram, Maine. Rent canoes with **Saco Bound Outfitters** and you can paddle for three hours to the put-out at Pigs Farm. Many paddlers will stop along the sandy shores to picnic and swim.

Ipswich River, Topsfield, Massachusetts

Snaking through the largest wildlife sanctuary in the Massachusetts Audubon Society, the Ipswich River is a bird lover's delight. **Foote Brothers Canoe Rentals** will drive you to the Salem Road put-in to begin a 7-mile jaunt back to the rental outpost. Ipswich is one of those narrow, serpentine rivers that was designed with a canoe in mind. The glass-like waters of the river is only interrupted by the occasional tree limb jutting up into the air. Snowy egrets usually stand tall in the marsh and the iridescent blue-green head of the common grackle searches for food on the banks.

Charles River, Boston, Massachusetts

Boston's Charles River is home to the Harvard crew team and hundreds of other rowers who yearn to be on the Harvard crew team. On a warm day in spring or fall, there are probably more sculls on the Charles than on the Thames in Oxford. This is especially true on the bend of the river between the Western Avenue and Eliot Bridges. **Charles River Canoe & Kayak** rents canoes and kayaks along the Charles in Boston, Cambridge, Waltham, Watertown and Newton to paddle.

5 Places to White Water Raft/ Kayak

Whitewater rafting is a thrilling experience that everyone can enjoy regardless of age or degree of shape. There's very little danger involved with these rafts, which easily handle high and rough water. Occasionally the craft will tip, but guides are experienced in assisting guests back into the boat, and everybody is required to wear a flotation device. To get the adrenaline pumping, try these rivers:

Kennebec River, The Forks, Maine

It was 1976 when intrepid outdoorsman Wayne Hockmeyer and a group of his friends braved the tumultuous Kennebec River in a twenty-foot raft. Prior to this time, the Kennebec was known solely for its fishing and the logs that went hurtling down the river to the mills below. When the Maine legislature passed a law prohibiting transportation of logs and pulpwood down the Maine rivers that summer, Hockmeyer opened **Northern Outdoors**. Get ready for a rip-roaring ride on Class III and IV rapids as the fast-moving river makes its way through a deep gorge.

Penobscot River, Millinocket, Maine

Moments after entering your raft and going over your first major rapid, Exterminator, you immediately realize this 14-mile stretch of the Penobscot is a serious joy ride that will have you shrieking with abandonment as the raft bends, turns, and twists backwards with every succeeding drop. On the backside of Mount Katahdin, every view is a winner. Minimum age is 12 on the Lower Penobscot, 15 on the Upper Penobscot.

Dead River, Eustis, Maine

It's a long drive on logging roads to reach the Spencer Rips put-in on the Dead River, but once there, be prepared for a glorious run on the longest stretch of continuous whitewater in New England. The river churns along 16 miles of almost nonstop Class III and IV rapids, enhanced by a half-dozen dam releases from May through October. There are no bridges, roads, or other signs of civilization until the end—just a rip-roaring ride through big water on rapids with names like Minefield, Humpty Dumpty, and Big Poplar Falls.

Deerfield River, Charlemont, Massachusetts

If you spend any amount of time in Williamstown or North Adams, Massachusetts, during the summertime, you'll notice all the cars traveling with kayaks tied to their roofs. They're all headed on Route 2 East, along the Mohawk Trail, to the surging Deerfield River in Charlemont. Dam releases by the New England Power Company cause rapids to tumble down two stretches of the river—the exhilarating Class IV rapids in the Dryway and the mellower Class II-III rapids farther south in the deep pools of Zoar Gap. Yet, you don't have to own a kayak to get a taste of New England whitewater. **Zoar Outdoor** take adrenalin junkies down the river in sturdy rafts.

West River, Jamaica, Vermont

Vermont's best whitewater run can be a zoo during the two days a year (the end of April and September) when the Army Corp of Engineers release the waters of the Ball Mountain Dam. The rest of the year, it can get a little dry, but it's still a scenic white-water kayaking run though the Green Mountains. The upper reaches should only be attempted by experienced paddlers with solid Class III skills. Soon the stream widens and slows down as you head towards the Connecticut River, allowing novice kayakers to do their thing. Good swimming holes and fishing are found at various points all along the West, including Jamaica State Park, about 2.5 miles down the river from the dam.

6 Places to Sail

Home to the America's Cup for more than 50 years, Newport and the rest of the northeastern Atlantic deserve their reputation as one of the leading cruising grounds in the world. Almost every day in summer, you'll see numerous rounded sails tacking in and out of legendary bays like Narragansett in Rhode Island and Penobscot off the mid-Maine coast. With reliable winds, there's hardly ever a luff. With hundreds of island anchorages, there are more than enough harbors in which to spend the day or evening. And let's not forget about the large lakes that lie inland— Champlain, Winnipesaukee, Moosehead, Squam, and many smaller bodies of water are just as popular with sailors. Also, a special shout out to the place I grew up sailing, Lake George. Not technically part of New England since it's located in upstate New York, I'm still going to include it because this is my book!

Newport, Rhode Island

The prevailing wind on Narragansett Bay is the "smoky sou'wester," the same breeze that drew the America's Cup races to Rhode Island for more than 50 years, until America's defeat by Australia in 1983. Almost without exception, calm sunny mornings are followed by windy afternoons with the onshore breeze arriving between 12 and 1 p.m. By mid-afternoon, the wind can build to 25 knots or more, but average speed is normally between 10 to 20 knots. Experienced sailors can rent J/22s and Rhodes 19s from **Sail Newport** at Fort Adams State Park. Novices can book a **34-foot O'Day with Sightsailing** and for two hours, be under the watchful of a knowledgeable captain who delivers an in-depth history of the region while tacking between the yachts and lighthouses.

Penobscot Bay, Maine

Maine's 2500-mile stretch of jagged coastline, where long inlets form sheltered bays, is tailor-made for sailing. No other sport gives you the freedom to anchor in a pristine cove, hike on an untrammeled island, and sleep with a lighthouse beacon as your nightlight. Yet, most people don't have the requisite experience to charter a sailboat. A viable alternative is to crew those schooners of yesteryear that line the mid-Maine coast, **the Windjammers**. It's hard to go wrong with any of these historic vessels, so choose whatever's available. Each boat has a story to tell. The Victory Chimes was built in 1900 in Bethel, Delaware, to carry lumber within Chesapeake Bay. Today, she's the only remaining three-masted schooner on the East Coast. The 92-foot American Eagle was built in 1930 as part of the Gloucester fishing fleet. It was revamped in 1984 and, along with Victory Chimes, Lewis R. French, and Stephen Taber are all National Historic Landmarks. Captains let passengers hoist the sails every day, even take the wheel to sail these big boys.

Boston Harbor Islands, Massachusetts

Sailing in Boston Harbor does have its distractions. Tugboats guide large oil tankers into the wharves and the jets flying into Boston's Logan Airport are so close that you can often see the rivets on the airplane's underside. Yet, that doesn't deter the hundreds of sailors who relish the opportunity on a clear day to find their own cruising ground in the water. The rewards are great. The wind is almost always at a good 10 to 20 knot clip. Boston's shimmering skyline is best seen from the water. And once you venture outside the port, traffic diminishes and you could very well find yourself picnicking on one of the deserted Boston Harbor Islands, home to the oldest continuously manned lighthouse in the country, a vintage Civil War fort, and many anchorages where you can have an island by your lonesome.

Buzzards Bay, Massachusetts

Every weekend in summer, cars flood Routes 195, 495, and 3 as they make their mass exodus to Cape Cod. Rarely will folks venture off the highway to explore the southeastern corner of Massachusetts because there's an urgency to cross the Sagamore and Bourne Bridges and not wait one additional minute. To the delight of those in the know, they leave behind places like Marion, Mattapoisett, and Padanaram that are very much like the Cape Cod of yesteryear. In the early 1800s, these small towns on the jagged coast of Buzzards Bay were the epicenter of the boatbuilding business, supplying whaleboats to crews in nearby New Bedford. Today, venturing out on the Atlantic is just as important, but for purely a recreational diversion. Yacht clubs dot the 280-mile stretch of Buzzards Bay. Grab a sloop and cruise to the Cape Cod shores in far more relaxed style than any highway. You can anchor off Wood's Hole for lunch before heading back or, if you prefer a quiet retreat, sail south to the Elizabeth Islands. A nice anchorage awaits at Tarpaulin Cove, on the south side of Nashon Island. With winds that average 10 to 15 knots daily, longer trips allow salty dogs to head to Martha's Vineyard, Nantucket, or further up the Cape to Chatham.

Burlington, Vermont

Approximately 120 miles long and 12 miles wide, Lake Champlain is the largest freshwater lake in the country after the Great Lakes. Consistently good wind, sheltered bays, hundreds of islands, and scenic anchorages combine to make this immense body of water one of the top cruising grounds in the Northeast. At the edge of Burlington Bay, **Let's Go Sailing** and **Whistling Man Schooner Company** both offer guided public and private sails. Once under sail, you'll be heading along the Vermont shores or toward the Adirondack Mountains that beckon you from the New York half of Champlain. Heading south, black cormorants fly overhead as you cruise past the luxurious houses of South Cove, Shelbourne Point peninsula, and sheltered Shelbourne Bay. Soon you'll reach the fertile fields of Shelbourne Farm. If you happen to tack to the middle of the lake, be sure to ask your Captain if he or she ever spotted "Champ," Lake Champlain's version of the Loch Ness Monster. The sea monster might very well be lurking from the depths.

Bolton Landing, New York

Most people associate Lake George with the honky-tonk town on its southern shores, Lake George Village. As a youngster growing up in these parts, I would beg my dad to stop here after a day of sailing, so I could spend my allowance in the arcades, play a round of **Goony Golf** (miniature golf), and down my fair share of soft-serve ice cream. Now it's my kids who plead with me to take them to Lake George Village while I crave the serenity of being on the water. The narrow lake is hemmed in by mountains on both sides, creating a placid oasis of verdant slopes and cobalt waters. Pick your mode of travel, via sailboat, sea kayak, motorboat, or aboard the paddlewheeler cruise ship, **The Mohican**. The middle section of the lake, just north of Bolton Landing, is blessed with numerous islands in the Narrows and Mother Bunch section. Day boaters congregate here for lunch, while campers can kiss away the woes of modernity as they breathe in the piney air for as long as their stay allows.

3 Places to Fish

From the trout and landlocked salmon caught in the Battenkill, Penobscot, and Kennebec Rivers, to the stripers, blues, cod, and tuna found in the Atlantic, you have to try hard not to hook anything in the waters of New England. Almost any body of water you venture to, whether it be a pond, river, lake, or ocean, you'll find an assortment of fish. But these are the places we've had the most fun dropping a line:

Surfcasting for Stripers, Martha's Vineyard, Massachusetts

There's a reason why saltwater fly fishing has outpaced all other categories of sport fishing the last several years. It's called striped bass. Found all along the New England coast, these fish have voracious appetites, grow to more than fifty pounds, and fight like champions. Striped bass, commonly referred to as stripers, can be found in remarkable numbers along the rips that lead from the ocean into the ponds of Martha's Vineyard. The beach south of the Edgartown Great Pond and Tisbury Great Pond are popular with local anglers. For expertise or gear, head to **Coop's Bait and Tackle**, 147 West Tisbury Road, near Edgartown. Cooper Gilkes is a third-generation islander who knows where the fish are biting.

Cape Cod's Kettle Ponds, Massachusetts

Don't overlook the freshwater fishing opportunities near the coast. The glacial kettles on Cape Cod are well-stocked. In early May, when the water temps hit the 50s, the fish start to bite. Flycasters wade in at Wellfleet's perfectly round Gull Pond to hook trout, smallmouth and largemouth bass, white perch, and pickerel. The pond is located a mile east of Route 6 on Gull Pond Road. The brown trout at Barnstable's Lovells Pond grow to robust sizes. At Nickerson State Park's Cliff Pond, a boat launch lets you troll slowly past schools of feisty rainbows and browns, while the smaller Flax and Little Cliff ponds are good for wading.

Flyfishing the Mettawee and White Rivers, Vermont

The Battenkill River has attained legendary status for the angler trying to hook the elusive trout. Yet, on the Vermont half of the river, the state refuses to stock the water, leading to a diminishing number of wild trout that are overfished and undermanaged. Thus the reason fly-fishermen who have spent years casting on the Battenkill now head to the nearby Mettawee. Northwest of Manchester, the Mettawee carves through farmland, a large stream that gets deeper as it approaches the ravines near New York. Gain access at any number of bridge crossings and you can spend a long morning here all by your lonesome. May and June are the prime months for hooking brown and brook trout, especially during the Hendrickson/Red Quill hatch in mid-Spring. For summertime fishing, head to the upper White River just south of Granville. Here, the mighty White is more like a narrow stream. Break out the hoppers or elk hair caddis and those rainbows will be striking hard. With a little luck and yes, some talent, a few might end up dangling from your hook.

3 Best Swimming Holes

I feel somewhat remorseful divulging these coveted swimming holes, but there's more than enough water to go around:

Bash Bish Falls, Mt. Washington, Massachusetts
At the northernmost tip of Mt. Washington State Forest on the New York state line, Bash Bish Falls is the largest waterfall in the state. Water cascades some 60 feet though a prism of rock to a deep pool below. In the summer months, families hike up to the falls and take a dip in the refreshing waters, ignoring the "No Swimming Allowed" signs. Nearby, on the New York side, is a wonderful bike path through farmland called the Harlem Valley Rail Trail. Many people combine the two for a perfect day outdoors. Camping is available at both Mt. Washington State Forest and the adjoining Taconic State Park in New York.

Williams Pond, Wellfleet, Massachusetts
If you drive the dirt Schoolhouse Hill Road, you reach a spit of land that separates Gull from Higgins Pond. Step out of your car and you'll find a narrow water passage cut through the land. This sluiceway, as it's called, was supposedly created by Native Americans to catch herring during their seasonal run. There are two parking spaces (stickers are necessary) to swim in Higgins, but the best mode of travel is via those

canoes on the shores of Gull Pond, rented by **Jack's Boat Rental**. Paddle into Higgins Pond and then onward to remote Williams Pond through another sluiceway. This is the place Henry David Thoreau visited a Wellfleet oysterman he would write about in his book, Cape Cod. It's also where architect and furniture designer Marcel Breuer built his house on the shores, camouflaged by the trees.

Directions: Take Route 6 into Wellfleet and turn right onto Gross Hill Road. A sharp left onto Gull Pond Road and Schoolhouse Hill Road will lead you to the parking lot.

Boulder Beach State Park, Groton, Vermont

There's nothing quite as therapeutic for both body and soul as a dip in a Vermont swimming hole, where the sylvan surroundings embrace you in a blanket of green. Nestled in one of Vermont's largest state forests in the northeast part of the state, Lake Groton is too large to be called a genuine Vermont swimming hole. There is no waterfall or covered bridge to swim under. In its place is a ring of mountains, with a forest of hemlocks, birches, and maples dropping all the way down to the lake's rim. The sand is nothing special, especially compared to its New England neighbors and their oceanfront setting. Ahh, but that cool refreshing lake water. Try it after a morning climb up 1,958-foot Owl's Head Mountain or a bike ride along the abandoned Montpelier-Wells River Railroad bed, and I guarantee that lake will be nourishing.

An Added Bonus!
Aerial Adventures, Tubing, Sculling, and Stargazing

Viewing the Night Sky from Sandy Pines Campground, Kennebunkport, ME

The largely rural state of Maine is known as one of the finest places in the nation to enjoy the night sky. Every September, Acadia National Park in Bar Harbor is home to Acadia Night Sky Festival, where workshops will teach you to become a constellation connoisseur and wow your friends back home. Head even further north to locales like Presque Isle and you might just catch a glimpse of the Northern Lights in the cooler months of the year. In late summer, we prefer the southern Maine coast town of Kennebunkport where a relatively new campground, **Sandy Pines**, offers guests a chance to go glamping in either comfy safari-style tents or cozy A-frames. Grab lobster rolls at their snack bar and stare at the stars from the expansive grounds, which also houses a general store, farm stand, ice cream cart, saltwater pool, kid's craft tent, playground, laundry facilities, spanking new bathrooms, and WiFi (SkyView Lite is a good app to help figure out constellations). Also check out the website of the Astronomical Society of Northern New England, based in Kennebunkport, to see if they have any special events happening during your stay.

Catamount Aerial Adventure Park, South Egremont, Massachusetts

Who can resist the chance to stand atop the tall maples and firs of the southern Berkshires, fly through the air on a tree rope a la Tarzan, and shriek with a mixture of fear and delight?

Allow a harness to be fitted to your body, hooking the carabineer, a metal coupling used by rock climbers, to the cables that line the trees atop the **Catamount Aerial Adventure Park**. After a brief introduction on how to use the equipment safely, you're handed a pair of gloves and off you go on this self-guided treetop obstacle course. The object is to simply reach the next platform which is not always so simple. Depending on which of the nine courses you choose, rated from easy to challenging like ski trails, you can zipline down a long cable, grab a trapeze swing and glide across a bridge on a snowboard, or try the rope swing, which offers an exhilarating feeling of freedom before being thrust into a web-like mesh.

Sculling Hosmer Pond, Craftsbury, Vermont

Sandwiched between the hills of Vermont's remote Northeast Kingdom, Hosmer Pond is the idyllic setting for the **Craftsbury Outdoor Center's sculling school**. If you ever wanted to learn the sport of sculling or already scull and want to perfect your stroke, Craftsbury is arguably the best place in the States to do just that. The class is usually a mix of novices and former crew members from the likes of Columbia and Yale. The weeklong course goes over all aspects of rowing, and depending on expertise, splits groups up on the lake with instructors. Balancing the boat is always the hardest part for beginners, many of whom will spend the better part of the first day swimming. Oar handles have to be together at all times or the boat quickly tips to the left or right. Legs are thrust up against a board to scoot back as you propel the oars forward. Indeed, many of the coaches have immense quad muscles proving that legs are more important than arms in the stroke. Those who use the rowing machine at the local gym know what a great workout sculling is for the whole body. It's far superior when you're outside, rowing on a lake and smelling the Vermont pines.

Tubing the Ogunquit River, Ogunquit, Maine

Ogunquit's 3 ½-mile wide stretch of beach is an ideal place to plop down your towel on a hot summer's day. That is, until you dip your toe in the Maine waters and realize this part of the Atlantic is a wee bit nippy. To cool off, head to the southernmost part of the beach, near the town center, and try Ogunquit's version of a lazy river. Halfway between high tide and low tide, the current of the Ogunquit River flows swiftly out to the Atlantic. Families wait patiently on the flat stretch of sand that rolls down to the river-bank. Once the current starts moving, the mass of beachgoers take the plunge—somewhat less chilly than the ocean but still an icy wake-up-call. Bring your favorite flotation device, be it an inner tube, boogie board, raft, or simply your back. Then get ready to giggle like a 5 year-old as the fast current carries you around the bend. The ride ends far too quickly as you wade through the shallow waters back to shore, contemplating another ride.

Winter Sports: 5 Retro Ski Resorts

The retro appeal has carried over to the mountains of New England, where folks are yearning for the skiing of yore. A time when people hand cut a sinuous line through a forest of birch, balsams and firs instead of the wide highway cruisers that have been shaved down the side of our favorite peaks in recent years. We want to feel what it's like to ride a single chairlift at Mad River Glen that's been hauling skiers up the slopes since 1948, to carve that perfect turn on snow-covered New Hampshire granite that's impervious to expansion, to slide down the only mountain on the Eastern seaboard with a view of the Atlantic in the backdrop. Well, here you go:

Camden Snow Bowl, Camden, Maine

Opened by the Camden Outing Club back in 1935, **Camden Snow Bowl** is the oldest ski area in the state and the only one still owned and operated by the town recreation department. It has the longest T-bar in Maine, which hauls you to the top of Ragged Mountain. Best of all, the Snow Bowl is the only place in America where atop the summit, skiers get ocean views. Gaze below at Camden's rock-strewn harbor and the islands that dot the Penobscot Bay—North Haven, Islesboro, and Matinicus, among others. Close proximity to the Atlantic also means that the weather can be iffy. The fog rolls in and the snow turns to mush. A nor'easter whips by and suddenly you're gleefully skiing in a blizzard. An added bonus, and possibly the main reason Snow Bowl is still around, is the 440-foot-long ice coated toboggan chute. Originally built in 1936, shut down in 1964, and reopened in 1991, this two-foot wide track will have the whole family shrieking as they drop off the side of the mountain at 30 miles per hour and glide halfway across Hosmer Pond.

Mad River Glen, Waitsfield, Vermont

Decades-old Subaru wagons with Vermont license plates often have a bumper sticker offering the following dare: "Mad River Glen, Ski It If You Can." No lie. **Mad River Glen** is the nastiest lift-served ski area in the East, a combination of rocks, ice, trees and snow, you hope. It's truly a place where skiing seems little removed from a mountain's gnarled, primal state. Think you're tough enough? Take the venerable single chair to the summit and start with Fall Line and Chute, two of the most precipitous, obstacle-strewn, yet perfect mogul runs you'll ever find. Next up is Grand Canyon, a steep mogul trail where the bumps are perfectly spaced. And for the finale—drum roll please—Paradise. Don't let the name fool you. Barely a trail, Paradise stumbles over rocky ledges and an enormous frozen waterfall to reach the bottom. Have fun trying to hold an edge. There is one obstacle that you don't have to worry about here. Mad River is the only major eastern ski area that does not allow snowboarding. And, yes, Mad River does have 14 beginner trails for the little ones when mom and dad are slicing it through the rough and tumble.

Middlebury College Snow Bowl, Ripton, Vermont

Even today, only one in four Middlebury College students opt for the season pass at their nearby ski hill. What they and other northeastern shredders are missing out on is one of the most scenic mountains in the region, where vistas are laden with ponds and red barns lost in the countryside. A place where poet Robert Frost found solace and inspiration. The skiing at the **Snow Bowl** isn't half-bad either. The frontside trails were cut in the 30s and 40s, some by Civilian Conservation Corp workers, so expect classic New England skiing where the soft greens turn to steep blacks at a moment's notice. More mellow cruisers are accessed from the Bailey Falls triple. The mountain is known for its extensive grooming, which critics say eliminates the bumps and lends itself to a far tamer mountain than need be.

Suicide Six, Pomfret, Vermont

Merely a fraction the size of its broad-shouldered neighbor to the west, Killington, **Suicide Six** is anything but a kitten of a mountain. At first glance, all you see is the wide black diamond Face trail falling sharply down the peak. When Bunny Bertram was looking for a place to put his ski area in 1936, he reportedly looked down this same hillside, then called Number 6, and said trying this is suicide. The name stuck. Take one of the two chairlifts to the top and you'll find a good mix of greens and blues that are hidden within the forest of pine. The Gully to Back Door and Double Dip is a sweet around-the-bend and zip down cruiser. Bunny's Boulevard is a wider run, but will still get the blood pumping. None of the trails are long. Comparable to other small Vermont ski areas like Middlebury Bowl and Mad River Glen, its intimacy and laid back attitude has made it a popular family venue for locals and flatlanders staying at the nearby Woodstock Inn & Resort, current owners of the ski area.

Butternut Basin, Great Barrington, Massachusetts

More than 50 years after Channing Murdock cut his first trail down the slopes of this Berkshire peak, **Butternut** remains a favorite for families. The Murdocks still own the area and the trails Channing cut continue to enchant a new generation of skiers who take delight at a particular stand of trees or vistas of the valley below. Geared to the beginner to intermediate skier, the runs are not very long (the longest being 1.5 miles) or scary. What you get are cruisers with decent switchbacks such as Freewheeler and Upper and Lower Applejack. Boarders have two terrain parks where they teach the youngins how to catch air.

8 Places to Cross-Country Ski

Lost in the woods, listening to my breath, I partake in one of winter's best cardio workouts. The blood is pumping, lungs are sucking in an endless supply of piney air, and all limbs are moving in fluid motion. Therein lies the appeal of cross-county skiing. I've had memorable outings at all of these locales:

Notchview, Dalton, Massachusetts
The Trustees of Reservations are best known as proprietors of beloved Crane Beach in Ipswich. Yet, the environmentally-sound organization maintains more than 100 sites across Massachusetts and some of their finest properties, like **Notchview Reservation**, in the western part of the state are best seen in winter. Notchview is a splendid 3,000-acre property, sheltered from winter winds by tall spruce and fir trees. The grounds boast 40 kilometers of cross-country skiing, almost half of that groomed, while side trails are favored by snowshoers. Start with Ant Hill Loop, where oaks and white pines, limbs heavy with snow, provide the perfect protection against the chilly winds. The half-mile trail is a gradual climb, guaranteed to leave you cozy by the time it drops you back off at the Circuit Trail. Take a quick right and then a left onto the Whitestone Trail, arguably the most scenic trail in the Berkshires. Especially on a day when the horizontal branches of the hemlocks

hold fresh snow, creating Mondrian-like right angles with the trunks, and a spectacular mesh of Malevich white-on-white wherever you look.

Blueberry Hill, Goshen, Vermont

In 1966, Tony Clark purchased an 1813 farm-house and parcel of land nestled deep within the Moosalamoo Region of Vermont's Green Mountain Range. Only 12 miles from Middlebury, the last four miles are on unpaved dirt roads, giving the inn an allure of being in the middle of nowhere. Clark has since built the 12-room **Blueberry Hill** into one of the most beloved inns in New England, known for its acres of cross-country and hiking trails, dinners around long tables, and an always ample supply of their signature chocolate chip cookies. The inn's cross-country ski center offers 75 km of trails providing good opportunity for all levels. There's the gently rolling Beginner Trail and the Hogback Trail that weaves in and out of pine and birch forests. More advanced skiers should opt for the Romance Trail. At an elevation of 3,000 feet, it's one of the highest groomed trails in Vermont.

Grafton Ponds, Grafton, Vermont

One of the few ski centers in New England that feature snowmaking, **Grafton Ponds** features a wonderful 5-kilometer loop even when there's no snow on the ground. If Mother Nature cooperates, you can add an additional 30 kilometers of groomed trails that start from the center's log cabin and winds through the forested hillside. Experienced Nordic skiers who make it up to the cozy Big Bear Shelter get their reward of hot chocolate and views of the historic village of Grafton below. Grafton Ponds also offers snow tubing down a 600-foot hill and skating on natural ponds. Afterwards, stop by the rustic Phelps Barn on the property of the **Grafton Inn**, plop down on one of the homey sofas and order a Vermont microbrew. You can toast to a great day of gliding atop the snow.

Trapp Family Lodge, Stowe, Vermont

With more than 400 km of interconnected ski trails, Stowe is the premier cross-country skiing destination in the northeast. Four of the top ski touring centers in New England are linked together, including **Trapp Family Lodge**, made famous by Maria von Trapp, whose family inspired The Sound of Music. Cross-country ski up to Slayton Pasture Cabin, a fantastic 10 km round-trip excursion, to earn your cup of soup next to the fireplace. Or better yet, visit during mid-March until mid-April, and you can cross-country ski to Trapp's sugarhouse. When it comes to making maple syrup, the von Trapps do it the old fashion way, picking up the sap in buckets with a horse-drawn sleigh and delivering it to the sugarhouse to boil off the water and create Vermont's "liquid gold." Come on Saturday during the sugaring season and you can participate in a traditional Sugar-on-Snow party. The hot syrup is tossed on the white snow to create a chewy maple taffy, served with donuts and dill pickles.

Darling Hill, East Burke, Vermont

Nestled atop a ridge between Lyndonville and East Burke is Darling Hill, a quintessential chunk of rolling farmland that happily satiates the romantic image you have of this bucolic state. Here, four immense red barns stand intact, forming a stark contrast with the snowy pasture. Built in 1883 by hotel owner Elmer Darling as the quintessential gentlemen's farm (and now part of the **Inn at Mountain View Farm**), the impressive barns once housed 100 Jersey cows, pigs, and Morgan horses. The meat and dairy products were shipped to Mr. Darling's Fifth Avenue Hotel in New York City. The Nordic Welcome Center is on 2079 Darling Hill Road in the Granary Building at the **Wildflower Inn**. There's more than 20 kilometers of groomed trails atop Darling Hill that rolls through the fields and connects the Inn at Mountain View Farm with the Wildflower Inn. For more advanced terrain, continue onto the Kingdom Trails system that snakes into the surrounding forest. Narrow trails sweep up and down the hills, shaded by fragrant spruces and firs.

Windblown XC, New Ipswich, New Hampshire

Only a 90-minute drive from Boston, southern New Hampshire's **Windblown** cross-country ski and snowshoe network has been a perennial favorite of the New England Nordic ski crowd since Al Jenks and his family debuted the 40 kilometers of trails in 1972. I park my car in the small lot, purchase a ticket and rent equipment in the handcrafted base lodge, and off I go, moving smoothly on the meticulously groomed terrain. Within moments, I'm immersed in a forest of tall pines, maples, and birches, staring at the steep slopes of Barrett Mountain, where the more intrepid skiers can play if need be. The scenery is inviting, a mix of small peaks, ponds, forest, and valley, one that a budding artist would want to sketch if they had the requisite pencil and paper.

Jackson Ski Touring Foundation, Jackson, New Hampshire

For sheer variety of trails, it's hard to top the **Jackson Ski Touring Foundation**, the largest cross-country skiing network in the northeast. Located in the historic hamlet of Jackson, over 100 miles of trails lead skiers away from the country inns and village green high up into the hills. The web includes the easy Ellis River Trail, which hugs a small brook, or the more the challenging Wildcat Valley Trail, created in the 1930s down the backside of the Wildcat Ski Area.

Bretton Woods Nordic Center, Bretton Woods, New Hampshire

Bretton Woods Nordic Center is on the grounds of the Omni Mount Washington Hotel, the grand dame of the White Mountains, over a century old. The expansive network features miles of groomed trails that cross over bridges and glide along streams on trails like Dark Forest, or veer down hills on the aptly named Coronary. Socked in a valley below New England's tallest peaks, the views couldn't be more spellbinding. 11 kilometers of dog-friendly trails ensure that all members of the family can join in on the fun.

Have Snowshoes, Will Travel

Venture out on a wintry day, when the trails are polished with a fresh dusting of snow, and you'll find snowshoers making their way up mountains, along the banks of a river, or strolling at the nearby golf course. Perhaps this recent surge of popularity stems from the ease of learning. "Strap and go" is how many folks describe the action of tying up the laces of the binding to your boots. Once attached, you're free to find your own "less-traveled" wilderness. Try these for starters:

Smugglers' Notch, Route 108, Stowe, Vermont

In the summer, Route 108 connects Stowe with the neighboring town of Jeffersonville, slicing through that exquisite mountainous pass they call Smugglers' Notch. Come winter, that same road is closed and only a handful of snowshoers in the know take advantage of that offering.

Snow has been falling for days when I enter and the tall pines feel the brunt of the deluge, bent over to create the raw and hardened look of winter. The scene becomes even more gripping as the road veers uphill and starts to twist. Sheer walls of quartzite and mica drop down to the large boulders resting on the floor below. The result is a notch formed by a glacial retreat over 10,000 years ago. I cross the road and continue on the rock steps up the side of a ridge, part of the Long Trail heading north. The views of the notch and surrounding Green Mountains get better with every steep step. At the top of the slope sits iced-over Sterling Pond, my picnic spot for the day.

The 19-Mile Brook Trail to Carter Notch, Pinkham Notch, New Hampshire

The Appalachian Mountain Club (AMC) keeps three of their huts in the Whites open in the winter. For snowshoers who relish a good climb, try the 3.8-mile (one-way) hike from Pinkham Notch to the **Carter Notch hut**. The 19-Mile Brook Trail will bring you to this special accommodation, situated between the dramatic ridges of Carter Dome and Wildcat "A." Here, you can spend the night at the AMC's oldest standing hut, a stone building constructed in 1914, perched just above two glacial lakes. The trail splits at the 1.8-mile mark, veering left to the top of Carter Dome or straight to Carter Notch. As you cross a bridge and continue the ascent to the notch, the northern hardwood forest is soon replaced by a boreal forest of sweet-smelling spruces and firs. The last section of the trail snakes between the ridges and the majestic glacial lakes to the old hut. Inside the cozy walls, you've earned your dinner and a night's sleep on a mattress.

Blue Hills Reservation, Milton, Massachusetts

Boston likes to call itself America's best walking town, but do locals really have a choice with a downtown infrastructure of rotaries and one-way streets that favor horse and buggies over cars? Serious walkers (and snowshoers) know there are some gems in the rough that start with the remarkable **Blue Hills Reservation**. 125 miles of trails criss-cross this 6,000-acre urban oasis. A favorite climb for young families leads to the observatory, with views of the buildings downtown. Snowshoers who like a challenge opt for the blue-blazed Skyline route, which leads you up Chickatawbut Hill before descending past Blue Hills Reservoir. When you reach the layers of granite known as The Crags, you can attempt to take the Crags Foot Path or simply retrace your steps on the Skyline back to the parking lot. Middlesex Fells Reservation in nearby Medford also has their version of the Skyline Trail (6.9 miles) with requisite view of downtown Boston. Far less traversed is a 6-mile loop around three of the Fells' reservoirs.

October Mountain State Forest, Lee, Massachusetts

With 16,500 acres to play, October Mountain State Forest is the largest green space in Massachusetts. One trip to these dense woods and hidden ponds and you realize why locals would like to keep this large tract of land a coveted secret. In winter, snowshoers can choose from a web of unplowed roads. One of the best is County Road. Simply park your car when the paved road ends, throw on your snowshoes, and continue for as long as your thighs and calves can endure. This is high plateau region with elevations ranging from 1,800 to 2,000 feet, so if there's snow anywhere in the state, it's a good chance you'll find it here. Hemlocks, spruces, birches, and oaks line the road like spectators at a marathon. An added bonus is the nine-mile stretch of the Appalachian Trail (ideally suited for families because of its relative ease) that pierces the heart of the forest.

Ten Mile Hill, Kent, Connecticut

The hikers who created the Appalachian Trail didn't just connect Georgia to Maine in a straight line from Point A to Point B. They created a sinuous path through the finest mountains and woods on the East Coast. This is especially true in the Litchfield Hills section of Connecticut where 53 miles of the AT weave through deep forests of maples, oaks, and hemlocks in the northwestern corner of the state. Part of the AT, the Ten Mile Hill trail starts at Bull's Bridge Falls. The trail rises above the water, before descending to Ten Mile Gorge. This is where the waters of the Housatonic and Ten Mile Rivers merge. From here, a series of switchbacks climb steadily to the crest of Ten Mile Hill. Up top, the westward view overlooks the Taconic Mountains, the Catskills in the distance, and the rolling farms in between.

6 Winter Adventures

Even as ski areas across New England make it more and more enticing to venture their way, adding an array of exciting activities like tubing and ziplining, many of us want to avoid the crowds in winter. We savor the opportunity to get lost in the wilderness, breathing in the scent of pines in relative quietude. Add a sport that will wipe away the mundane worries of the world and you'll quickly remember why we live in New England during the cool winter months. If these options don't get you excited, nothing will!

Two Nation Snowmobile Vacation, Presque Isle, Maine

An hour's drive north of mighty Mount Katahdin in Baxter State Park, you reach the top tier of Maine and Aroostook County, the largest county east of the Mississippi River. Simply called "The County" by Mainers, Aroostook is known as the potato-growing capital of the East. Come winter, however, those potato fields connect to long dormant railroad corridors, seemingly endless logging roads through dense forest, and iced-over lakes and rivers to create a mind-boggling 2300 miles of snowmobile trails. But that's not all. Simply bring a passport and you can cross into the province of New Brunswick, and add another 4,000 miles of trail, half of which flows through state forests and parks.

Start your two-nation adventure in Presque Isle, a town of 10,000 people that serves as the economic hub of The County. Stay at the Presque Isle Inn, where next door is **Kevin Freeman's Sled Shop**. Freeman, a former professional snowmobile racer has logged more than 250,000 miles on snowmobiles in the region so he knows the routes like the back of his hand. He can send you off with a detailed map or guide you for the day. He can also equip you with insulated snowmobile pants, jacket, and helmet, and line the 110 horsepower Ski-Doo with panniers, so you can bring all the necessities for an overnight in Canada.

Head directly across Main Street from the Sled Shop and you're heading west on ITS (Interconnecting Trail System) 85. This is not a situation where you're knocking on a farmer's door asking how to get home. Signage is excellent and routes are well-maintained by more than 40 dedicated snowmobile clubs in the area. If you happen to hit a trail just after being groomed, it's like driving a Mercedes on the Autobahn.

On a 250-mile weekend jaunt, head west to Portage Lake and have lunch at Dean's, a favorite snowmobile stop known for their fish and lobster stews. Don't miss ITS 105, leading northeast from Washburn to Stockholm, a narrow and level railroad corridor where you can easily reach speeds of 75 miles per hour. Go too fast, however, and you'll miss the moose, deer, snowy owls, and the rare white ermine that call this forest home.

At Hamplin, go through Customs on snowmobile and spend the night at the nearby Quality Inn in Grand Falls. The next morning, wake up and savor the long suspension bridge that glides above the St. John River. Then make your way to the New Brunswick interior on logging roads past mills and on railroad beds where snowed-over balsams stand like spectators at a marathon. The quaint French village of Saint-Quentin is a good place to grab lunch and gas up before making the return trek back across the border to Presque Isle.

Cost of snowmobile rental is $250 per day.

Cross-Country Ski Hut-to-Hut in Carrabassett Valley, Maine

Maine Huts & Trails is a nonprofit organization determined to build 12 backcountry huts over 180 miles of trails in the remote western mountains of the state. They recently unveiled their fourth property, Stratton Brook, overlooking the 4,000-foot peaks of Carrabassett Valley. When the 180-mile route is complete, it will be the longest groomed ski trail in America. Yet, there's no need to wait. This winter, you can choose from a variety of options, from staying at one of the four comfortable lodgings and going out on daily excursions, or self-guided or guided cross-country ski trips that lead from one hut to the next. Each of the four huts is spaced about 11 miles apart, so people can reach it within one day of cross-country skiing or snowshoeing. The ultimate adventure is a four-night/five-day package that includes 50 miles of skiing and spending each night at a different property. All meals, shuttle of gear, and lodging are included in the price.

Dogsled Umbagog Lake on the Maine/New Hampshire Border

Polly Mahoney and Kevin Slater, owners of **Mahoosuc Guide Service**, have chosen a good base for their dogsledding operations. They live on the outskirts of Grafton Notch State Park in the heart of the Maine woods. Almost every weekend in winter, Polly and Kevin, with 15 of their dogs, drive some 30 miles to the remote shores of Umbagog Lake. Here, guests learn the basics of the sport—standing on the back of the sled and shouting the magic words "Let's go!" (never "Mush") to see the dogs romp through the snow or yelling "Whoa!" to slow the dogs down. You'll take turns dogsledding and cross-country skiing on iced-over lakes, fringed by mountains of pines. At night, you'll sleep in heated tents on a floor of cushiony fir needles, only to awake to the sounds of the dogs howling in the pre-dawn hours. Polly breeds her own type of dog, which she calls a Yukon husky. A native Mainer, she spent a decade learning her trade in the Yukon bush. She returned home and met Kevin at a nearby Outward Bound center when he was in dire need of a skilled dogsledder. Two and three-day outings include food, tents, sleeping bags, even cozy parkas, mukluks, and leg gaiters.

Hike and Ski at Tuckerman Ravine, Pinkham Notch, New Hampshire

Expert skiers who want to carve some turns away from the masses should head to a mountain that has no towropes, T-bars, or even super quads. Tuckerman Ravine is a large glacial cirque on the southeast shoulder of Mount Washington that fills up with snow from the mountain's summit. By springtime, this natural amphitheater is ready for skiers to cut their line down some of the steepest pitches in the country. "Tuck" should only be attempted by expert downhill and telemark skiers. The rest of us will find it just as exciting to watch the spectacle. In 1932, the U.S. Forest Service constructed a Fire Trail from behind the **AMC Pinkham Notch Visitors Center**. This is still the only way to get to Tuckerman today. Called the Tuckerman Ravine Trail, it is an unrelenting, 2.4-mile, two-hour climb to Hermit Lake Cabin or HoJo's, as regulars call it, and another 0.7 mile to the base of the ravine. Throw on a fresh pair of polypropylene up top so you don't freeze. Then decide your destiny. You can ski Left Gully, Right Gully, or the longest run, Hillman Highway. Pitches range from 35 to 55 degrees depending on the trail you choose. It's wise to talk to other skiers to see which trail has the best snow and is the easiest to climb. On a sunny spring day, hundreds of spectators and skiers congregate on the Lunch Rocks. These large boulders on the lower right side of the headwall are the place to cheer on crazed skiers.

Ice Fishing Harriman Reservoir, Wilmington, Vermont

Take a drive on southern Vermont's Route 9 during the winter and you'll undoubtedly see numerous snowmobilers whipping across the ice of Harriman Reservoir. They're not out for a joy ride. These hearty souls eventually find a spot to stop and put up their shanties before getting out their small poles and start jigging for fish. Just outside of Wilmington and the Mt. Snow region, Harriman is one of the best ice fishing holes in New England. Expect to find browns (29-pounders are not unheard of), brookies, rainbows, landlocked salmon, perch, and pickerel.

Earle's Bait Shop in Guilford (off I-91) sells jigs, poles (22-26 inch poles are the norm), fresh bait (minnows), and can order ice shanties ($200-$300). Some of the old-timers are so adept at ice fishing that they line their shanties with generators and TVs.

Snowboarding the Backcountry, Stowe, Vermont

Vermont's David Goodman certainly knows how to take advantage of the snow. As author of Best Backcountry Skiing in the Northeast: 50 Classic Ski Tours in New England and New York (AMC), Goodman has spent the past 30 years writing about backcountry terrain. A personal favorite for Goodman are the trails that were hand-cut by the Civilian Conservation Corp in the 1930s creating the first ski trails down Vermont's tallest peak, Mount Mansfield. When Stowe Ski Area was introduced, many of these gems were forgotten until Goodman and others brought them back to the forefront again. They include Teardrop, a characteristic backcountry New England ski trail, featuring glimpses of the mountains as you twist and turn on a narrow trail. Around every bend is another surprise, be it the vista or an abrupt change of course.

Lately, Goodman has being seeing a growing legion of snowboarders on the trails. Like skiers, they come to the backcountry for the wilderness experience and the chance to test their skills on powder. At ski resorts, you have to wake up early to get your own coveted pocket of powder, because locals rise before the sun and hit the trails hard. The backcountry offers far more accessibility to deep snow. Boarders have the choice of simply snowshoeing up and snowboarding back down or splitboarding, cutting your snowboard in two and attaching skins to cross-country ski up the hill. At the top, you snap your board together with bindings and head back down.

For the History and Culture Junkie

5 Best Spots to Relive History

The first established settlement in New England, Plymouth, was founded in 1620, a mere 150 years before the start of the Revolutionary War. So it comes as no surprise that folks visit this region of America to see how the country first laid down its roots. There are the obvious sights like the Freedom Trail and other not so obvious sights that history lovers will cherish like the Shelburne Museum. Have a look:

Freedom Trail, Boston, Massachusetts

Follow the **Freedom Trail** and its distinctive red brick line into some of Boston's most cherished neighborhoods—Beacon Hill's century-old brownstones and village squares, North End's winding streets, and Charlestown, once the site of the Battle of Bunker Hill and now home to the Bunker Hill Monument, an obelisk to commemorate this historic Revolutionary fight and America's most celebrated ship, the U.S.S. Constitution. Two of the most important sites of the American Revolution are the Old South Meeting House and the Old State House. On December 16, 1773, some 7,000 citizens came to Old South, spilling out into the streets to protest the Tea Act. When the British refused for the final time to take their tea back home, Samuel Adams rose and said, "Gentlemen, this meeting can do nothing more to save the country." Thus, the start of the Boston Tea Party.

The first bloodshed of the Revolution took place just outside the Old State House. Known as the Boston Massacre, five colonists were killed when a squad of British officers fired into a taunting, jeering mob. Another highlight is Old North Church, where Paul Revere's good friend, Robert Newman was instructed to hang lanterns from the steeple windows to tip off how the British redcoats were arriving: "One, if by land, and two, if by sea." By sea was the chosen route and, once alerted, Revere would quickly paddle across the Charles River, mount a horse and race west. The night was April 19, 1775, and it would lead to the official start of the Revolutionary War.

Minute Man National Historic Park, Lexington and Concord, Massachusetts

Start your tour of **Minute Man National Historic Park** at the Visitors Center, where a 30-minute film gives a good overview of the remarkable events that day. Then continue along Route 2A into Concord, to see where Paul Revere was captured by the British (they took his horse but surprisingly let him go) and onward to historic North Bridge, where local militia confronted the large British regimen. After the British fired and killed two colonists, the militia returned gunshots. It was not only an act of treason against the British government, but it ended up killing the first British soldiers and became known "as the shot heard round the world." By the end of that bloody day, 73 British soldiers would die alongside 49 colonists.

New Bedford Whaling National Historic Park, New Bedford, Massachusetts

The 13-block radius of the **New Bedford Whaling National Historic Park** (the Visitor Center is located at 33 Williams Street) speaks of a time in America when whale oil was worth its weight in gold. At the Whaling Museum (18 Johnny Cake Hill), a 65-foot-long skeleton of the largest whale, the blue, hangs from the ceiling. The museum's centerpiece is a half-scale replica of the whaleboat, Lagoda, built in 1916 and still the largest ship model in existence. The original Lagoda was built in 1826 and sailed the seas for more than 60 years. Across the street from the museum is the white steepled chapel known as Seamen's Bethel (15 Johnny Cake Hill). Melville came to this small church and was so amazed by the chaplain of the time, the passionate Reverend Enoch Mudge, that he created a character based on him in Moby Dick. The walls are covered with memorial tablets to whalers and fishermen who have died in every watery corner of the globe. Cenotaphs from the 1840s hang side-by-side with more recent memorials from the 1980s and 90s. One reads "In Memory of Captain W. M. Swain, The Master of the Christopher Mitchell. This worthy man after fast'ning to a whale, was carried overboard by the line, and drowned. May 19, 1844, in the 49th year of his age."

The Mansions, Newport, Rhode Island

Equipped with an audio tour to go as fast or slow as you want, all ages will enjoy a visit to the **Newport mansions**. These "summer cottages" were no rustic cabins in the woods. They were fifty to seventy room estates with large stables, spacious lawns, gardens, and greenhouses, immense palaces of marble, limestone, and granite. Start with The Breakers. Constructed in 1895 for railroad tycoon Cornelius Vanderbilt, it took more than two years and a hundred workers to complete the building. Unfortunately for Vanderbilt, he died three years after his dream house was finished. Back on Bellevue Street, you'll pass Chateau-sur-Mer, built for William Wetmore who amassed a fortune in the China trade, William and Alva Vanderbilt's sumptuous Marble House, and Rosecliff, the famed mansion designed by the illustrious architect Stanford White in 1900 and seen in the film, The Great Gatsby.

Shelburne Museum, South Burlington, Vermont

Kids and their parents will love the impressive collection of 150,000 objects collected by Electra Havemeyer (1888-1960) and housed in 37 buildings at the **Shelburne Museum**, seven miles south of Burlington. The buildings themselves are museum pieces, having been moved here from other parts of New England to save them from the bulldozer. Highlights include a sawmill (1786), covered bridge (1845), lighthouse (1871), a luxury private rail coach (1890), historic round barn (1901), an authentic Lake Champlain side-wheeler steamboat, the SS Ticonderoga (1906), even a railroad station complete with locomotive (1915). Art exhibitions include works by renowned 19th and early 20th-century painters Claude Monet, Mary Cassatt, Edgar Degas, Winslow Homer, and Grandma Moses.

11 Best Art Museums

Blame it on the majestic scenery in New England that lured artists to its shores and mountains, or savvy collectors who had the foresight to purchase the preeminent works of their time. The result is undeniable. The bounty of art found in this region is mind-boggling, from the American art collection at the Museum of Fine Arts, Boston, to the Hudson River School paintings hanging at Hartford's Wadsworth Athenaeum to the Impressionist gems located at the Clark Art Institute in Williamstown, Massachusetts. Add university collections like Harvard's Fogg and Yale's Center for British Art that could rival the finest art museum in most mid-range cities, and you understand how spoiled we are.

The Museum of Fine Arts, Boston, Massachusetts
The MFA's permanent collection is an encyclopedic offering, second only to New York's Metropolitan Museum of Art for its quantity of art in the country. Designed by such architectural luminaries as Guy Lowell and I.M. Pei, the massive building increased in size in 2010 with the emergence of the American Wing, a $500 million expansion. Head straight to the galleries on early American painting to find Gilbert Stuart's well-known portrait of debonair George Washington, along with John Singleton Copley's painting of Paul Revere. Few realize that Revere

was a silversmith, yet next to his portrait is a large collection of his own wares. Other favorites in the MFA are John Singer Sargent's Daughters of Edward Darley Boit (1882), an icon of childhood, where each of the four girls are scattered around the canvas like chess pieces and have their own honest response to the painter; and Paul Gauguin's masterpiece Where Do We Come From? What Are We? Where Are We Going? (1897-1898). "I believe that this canvas not only surpasses all my preceding ones, but that I shall never do anything better," Gauguin wrote after completing the large Tahitian work. It's hard to disagree, after getting lost in that lush green background.

The Harvard Art Museums, Cambridge, Massachusetts

Home to 35 colleges and more than 150,000 college students each semester including Boston University and Boston College, Boston is best known for those two universities across the Charles River in Cambridge, Harvard and MIT. Enter Harvard Yard to visit the venerable halls of learning, stopping at the John Harvard sculpture to touch his shiny foot for good luck. Then visit the recently renovated **Fogg Museum** to see their excellent collection of pre-Raphaelite works, and the Harvard Museum of Natural History, home to a rare collection of glass flowers.

Peabody Essex Museum, Salem, Massachusetts

The highlight of any trip to Salem is the chance to view some of the vast collection of art found at the **Peabody Essex Museum**. Founded over two centuries ago, the Peabody has a wealth of wares from China, Japan, Korea, India, the Pacific Islands, and Africa, not to mention vast holdings of Native American crafts, New England Maritime Art, and 18th and 19th-century dwellings from Salem's historic streets. The quandary here has always been how to display some 2.5 million objects when they only have space to show two percent of their holdings. Don't miss venturing into the Yin Yu Tang House on the first floor. Originally built between 1800 and 1825, this Chinese merchant's house was purchased whole from ancestors of the original family and sent piece by piece to Salem. You'll visit the bedrooms, kitchen, and inner courtyard while hearing stories about the family on a self-guided audio tour.

Worcester Art Museum, Worcester, Massachusetts

A little over a century ago, American artists began to paint with loose, rapid strokes in the striking manner of Impressionism, the French movement that had begun two decades earlier. One of their favorite places to exhibit their work was the thriving industrial city of Worcester. There the new **Worcester Art Museum** held yearly juried shows and awarded prizes to the finest artists. Today, the Worcester Art Museum houses one of the finest American Impressionist collections in the world. Walk into the imposing building and you'll be awed by the works of Mary Cassatt, John Singer Sargent, Childe Hassam, and William Merritt Chase. The latest addition to the Worcester Art Museum is the acquisition of the Higgins Armory Museum and their intriguing collection of armor and arms.

Wadsworth Athenaeum, Hartford, Connecticut

One glance of Georgia O'Keeffe's ultra sensual Slightly Open Clam Shell (1926) and you'll never look at a bucket of steamers the same way again. The pastel is part of 100 works on paper from the **Wadsworth Athenaeum**'s collection. Spanning 50 years, from 1910 to 1960, you'll find a whole wall devoted to Edward Hopper, an unknown entity when the Wadsworth rewarded the artist with his first solo show in 1928. Also in the collection are wonderfully whimsical surrealist works by Yves Tanguy and Salvador Dali. The Wadsworth is best known for its collection of 19th-century master-pieces by Thomas Cole, Frederick Church, and Albert Bierstadt. A sampling of Hudson River School Artists' works can be found in the renovated galleries near the main lobby and should not be missed.

Yale Center for British Art, New Haven, Connecticut

The Yale Center for British Art is home to the largest repository of British art outside of the UK. Hogarth, Gainsborough, and Turner are just a few of the well-known Brits on display. The building stands across from architect Louis Kahn's other major commission on campus, the equally impressive **Yale University Art Gallery**.

Norman Rockwell Museum, Stockbridge, Massachusetts

Norman Rockwell (1894-1978) lived and worked in Stockbridge for the last 50 years of his life. During that time, he would create 321 covers for the Saturday Evening Post, as well as illustrations for books, posters and many other magazines, easily becoming the most popular illustrator in American history. **The Norman Rockwell Museum** houses over 200 of his best known works, including the beloved Triple Self-Portrait (1960). Here, his keen sense of humor is evident as an older Rockwell looks in a mirror only to paint a much younger version of himself.

Clark Art Institute, Williamstown, Massachusetts

Head to the **Clark** and you'll no doubt walk away stunned, wondering how come you've never heard of this relatively unknown treasure chest of art. There are Impressionist paintings by Monet, Degas, Pissarro, and no fewer than 30 Renoirs. American artists are well represented by rooms of Homers, Sargents, and Remingtons. There are even several works by such masters as Goya and Turner.

Mass MoCA, North Adams, Massachusetts

Art lovers should start their tour of the northern Berkshires in the industrial town of North Adams, where you'll find **Mass MoCA**, the largest center for contemporary art in the United States. It took 12 years to transform the buildings of the former Sprague Electric Company into an art extravaganza that now spans 26 buildings across 16 acres. The latest addition in 2017 includes works by light artist James Turrell, whose pieces bathe the rooms in hypnotic colored lights. Be sure to also spend time at Building 7, devoted entirely to the massive wall drawings of the late painter Sol Lewitt. The show opened in November 2008 and will be on display for 25 years.

Portland Museum of Art, Portland, Maine

The rugged and raw beauty of Maine has been a lure to many of America's foremost landscape artists. Thomas Cole, founder of the Hudson River School, first visited Mount Desert Island in 1844. When he returned home to New York with a bounty of canvases, Cole's affluent patrons were astounded by the mix of mountains and sea. Man versus the chaotic forces of nature, particularly fishermen struggling against powerful nor'easters, kept Winslow Homer busy on the boulder-strewn shores of Prouts Neck for more than two decades. In the 1920s, Georgia O'Keeffe, Marsden Hartley, and other early American abstractionists from Alfred Stieglitz's 291 Gallery joined John Marin to work at his summer cottage in Deer Isle. Marin's unique use of loose impressionistic strokes and abstract patterns captured the imagery of Deer Isle, situated halfway up the Maine coast. Maine has been fortunate to keep a good sampling of these artists' works in the state thanks to collectors who have bequeathed their works to local museums. The **Portland Museum of Art** has more than 250 of Winslow Homer's illustrations and a strong collection of Homer, Marin, and Hartley paintings.

The Farnsworth, Rockland, Maine

Monhegan Island has been a favorite subject of Jamie Wyeth, whose father Andrew Wyeth and grandfather N.C. Wyeth all summered on the Maine coast. Indeed, Andrew met his wife and her best friend Christina Olson in Maine. Olson is the woman lying down in the tall grass of Wyeth's iconic painting,

Christina's World. At the **Farnsworth Museum** in Rockland, a 19th-century Methodist church has been transformed in the Wyeth Center. A vast collection of works by three generations of Wyeths are on display. In nearby Cushing, you can visit the farmhouse Andrew Wyeth painted as a backdrop in Christina's World (see Hidden Art Historical Gems below).

6 Hidden Art Historical Gems

Blessed with this bevy of art, you shouldn't be surprised that there are some hidden treasures to be found in the region. Several of these picks have been recently refurbished, acquired National Historic Landmark status, or simply added better lighting to enhance the presentation of the works. There's no time like the present to check them out:

The Olson House, Cushing, Maine

Veer off Route 1 in Thomaston, Maine, onto River Road and you soon enter the small community of Cushing and its rich tapestry of rolling meadows, sheltered coastal inlets, and faded red barns. This varied terrain and its inhabitants were the perfect fodder for the canvases of Andrew Wyeth. The artist would create more than 70 paintings in his lifetime just from the scenery along River Road, yet it's **the former 18th-century sea captain's house on Hathorne Point Road** that would become the backdrop for his most famous work, Christina's World (1948). On the same day Wyeth met his soon-to-be wife, Betsy James, she introduced them to two friends, sister and brother Christina and Alvaro Olson. Walk inside the house to the smell of old wood, seasoned by the salty air, and find farming equipment used by Alvaro, the wood stove that did its best to heat the structure on harsh winter nights, and a vase of fresh geraniums, placed exactly as they were during the Olson's lifetime, right next to the rocking chair.

Then stroll outside to the front yard to find the meadow where Christina Olson is found in the forefront of the iconic painting now housed in New York's Museum of Modern Art. At first glance, Christina seems to be reclining in the tall grass, but then we learn that the woman is actually crawling. Stricken with polio, she had no use of her legs. Wyeth once wrote, "The challenge to me was to do justice to her extraordinary conquest of a life which most people would consider hopeless." Finish your tour of the property across the street to see where Wyeth is buried, and then down the road to the Cushing docks, where lobstermen sell their fresh catch to anyone who stumbles upon them.

Winslow Homer Studio, Prouts Neck, Maine

Acquired in 2006 by the Portland Museum of Art, **Homer's former home** reopened after the Museum poured in more than $10 million restoring the structure to its original intention. A refinished piazza and copper roof are just some of the touches added to Homer's main residence from 1883 until his death in 2010. A tour inside will reveal the watercolors his mother painted, a sign he created, "SNAKES! SNAKES! MICE!" to dissuade his growing fan club from interrupting his work, his signature etched into one of the glass windows, and the worn second-story floorboards where he paced back and forth to view his beloved Atlantic seascape. The interior is dark, with very little natural light, and the studio feels claustrophobic, even after spending just a few minutes inside. The monastic conditions suited the painter perfectly, since it only forced him to be outside as much as possible, atop Prouts Neck's craggy coastline that serves as a frothy welcome mat to the fury of the sea.

Take Homer's cue and stroll atop the mile-long cliff walk and you'll be entering some of his most famous paintings. To the left, a cylindrical rock juts out of the shoreline, similar to the formation in Cannon Rock (1895, Metropolitan Museum of Art). Soon the trail starts its ascent, offering glorious ocean vistas, and Homer's inspiration for High Cliff, Coast of Maine (1894, National Gallery of Art). The artist cherished the off-season, the time of year when nasty nor'easters and powerful gales would wreak havoc on this spit of land, leading to his most vivid paintings. Thankfully, the Portland Museum of Art will also avoid the summer months, offering tours of the studio during spring and fall.

St. Johnsbury Athenaeum, St. Johnsbury, Vermont

With its requisite Irving gas station, diner, and red-brick paper mill, St. Johnsbury at first glance looks like any other small industrial town in northern New England. But then you head up a hill to Main Street, and the opulence of yesteryear starts to seep into the picture. Churches share the street with the class-rooms of St. Johnsbury Academy and grand Victorian homes, including the mansard-roofed public library called the **St. Johnsbury Athenaeum**. By all means, pull over, as I have countless times to the sheer delight of any passenger held captive in my car. Enter the library, past rows of leather-bound books, to the back room. Sunshine filters in from the cupola skylight onto the parlor chairs and black walnut floors, illuminating the more than 100 paintings that line the red walls of America's oldest art gallery. Built in 1873, many of the gilded-framed works here are by prominent Hudson River School painters like Asher B. Durand, Sanford Gifford, and Jasper Cropsey. Yet, the crowning achievement of the collection is the immense piece of art that fills the entire back wall of this small space, Albert Bierstadt's 10-by-15-foot panorama, Domes of Yosemite.

When this mountainous vista of Yosemite Falls was first painted in 1867, the New York Times stated that it was "worth a week's travel to see this great picture." Bierstadt was paid the then-exorbitant sum of $25,000 to create the piece for Connecticut financier Legrand Lockwood. Lockwood would soon go bankrupt and die, forcing his widow to sell Domes at auction to the architect of the St. Johnsbury Athenaeum. "Now the Domes are doomed to the seclusion of a Vermont town, where it will astonish the natives," the Boston Globe first reported in 1872. We know, however, that the Athenaeum did receive one out-of-town visitor. Albert Bierstadt returned to the gallery every summer until his death to touch up his masterpiece.

Baker Library, Dartmouth College, Hanover, New Hampshire

In the spring of 1932, Dartmouth College made the shrewd move of inviting renowned Mexican muralist,

Jose Clemente Orozco, to their campus to lecture and demonstrate his style of fresco painting. In a hallway inside the **Baker Library**, he created a work based on the Greek figure, Daedelus, where a man rises from the wreckage of machinery. The finished piece would be a prized example that would quickly lead to a major commission for Orozco, the chance to paint the walls of the new Baker Library reading room at Dartmouth. The artist accepted the challenge and for the next two years he would paint 24 massive panels, eschewing his original mythological theme for a much headier concept, the combined influence of indigenous and European cultures on America. Titled The Epic of American Civilization, the work is now considered by art critics as one of the two most influential Mexican murals in America, along with Diego Rivera's Detroit Industry at the Detroit Institute of Art.

Orozco's masterpiece is a scathing critique of humanity, which led to much controversy when it was unveiled in 1934 and feels just as bold today. He used the symmetry of the space to devote panels on the West Wing to Mesoamerican themes, and the East Wing to the growing European power. The panels jump from discordant concepts like human sacrifice to harmonious ideals like the Pre-Columbian golden age of agriculture, arts, and sciences. No subject was spared Orozco's scorn, from nationalism to religion to education. One panel in particular, Gods of the Modern World, must have had Dartmouth professors up in arms. Skeletons dressed in academic garb look on indifferently as another skeleton gives birth to "dead knowledge."

New London Post Office, New London, Connecticut

Upon entering the New London post office, you might feel silly peering at art while other folks are standing in line to send off packages. Bring in a letter if you have to, but don't let that dissuade you from visiting this cavernous edifice, almost a block long in the heart of downtown New London. Atop the P.O. Boxes are six panels of a mural completed by Thomas LaFarge in 1938. At the height of the Great Depression, LaFarge won a competition and became one of the growing numbers of New Deal muralists hired by the Federal Government "to provide work for all Americans, including artists." LaFarge's winning theme on whaling was perfectly suited for a community that was built on the backbone of baleen.

To the right of the Masonic Street entrance, you'll find the two panels of Aloft (all six panels are exactly the same dimension, 3 feet wide by 14 ½ feet long). A shirtless sailor climbs the mainsail, strapping and as formidable as this building. On the adjacent mural, a long line of men work in tandem to hoist a sail, an uplifting message for Americans that we're going to get through these hard times by toiling together. LaFarge was an avid sailor but whaling was not his expertise. Several "old salts" still living in New London when he made his preliminary sketches, questioned the anatomy of his whale. The large mammal was left out of the two panels titled "Cutting In," where another brawny sailor digs his harpoon into the water. The artist, a grandson of John LaFarge, the man who created the exquisite stained glass windows in Boston's Trinity Church, would soon commandeer his own ship, a Coast Guard cutter, during World War II. In 1942, the ship went down off the coast of Newfoundland and LaFarge would die at the young age of 38, leaving these whaling murals as his legacy.

Weir Farm National Historic Site, Wilton, Connecticut

When New York City collector Erwin Davis became obsessed with a painting owned by artist Julian Alden Weir, he gave him an offer that was hard to refuse. In exchange for the painting and ten dollars, Davis would transfer over the deed to a 153-acre farm less than an hour outside of New York in the Connecticut countryside. Weir arrived in the summer of 1882, immediately became enamored with the sylvan setting, and painted the first of hundreds of works he and his friends would create over the next 40 years. To this day, the property remains a rural retreat that continues to inspire artists and is now **the only site in the National Park System dedicated to American painting**. Walk inside the Visitor Center to see a short film on the life J. Alden Weir, considered one of the fathers of American Impressionism. That's not to say he wasn't disgusted with this style of painting when he first encountered it in Paris, calling an exhibition showcasing the works of Monet, Manet, and Degas "worse than the Chamber of Horrors." Yet, soon enough, Weir was utilizing the loose brushstrokes and plein air painting that would become the trademarks of Impressionism.

View the wonderful photographs of Weir with John Singer Sargent and Childe Hassam, two of the celebrated artists that enjoyed visiting Weir at his country home, and see the lone original work in the building, The Truants (1895). Then immerse yourself in the same natural setting that inspired Weir. Trails lead to a pond, barns, old stone walls, a sunken garden, and his house and studio. Better yet, bring a sketchbook.

4 Best Literary Landmarks

Yes, we have our fair share of renowned authors too.

Mark Twain House, Hartford, Connecticut

In 1873, Samuel Clemens, otherwise known as Mark Twain, purchased a large plot of land on Farmington Avenue in Hartford, Connecticut. The cost of building his home went quickly over budget, but the family moved in the following year. Twain would live here until 1891 and would write two of his most famous books in this house, Adventures of Huckleberry Finn (1884) and A Connecticut Yankee in King Arthur's Court (1889). Today, the **Mark Twain House** is open to the public and is one of the last remaining interiors designed by Louis Comfort Tiffany.

Harriet Beecher Stowe House, Hartford, Connecticut

Harriet Beecher Stowe's humble abode is just a short stroll away from Mark Twain's house, under the tall hemlocks and past the expansive magnolia tree. Stowe moved here in 1873 with her preacher husband long after she had experienced world acclaim for writing Uncle Tom's Cabin as well as the depths of sorrow from the drowning of her 19-year old son on the Dartmouth, New Hampshire campus. Walk into the front parlor and peer at the many watercolors around the room and you'll soon realize that

Stowe was also an accomplished artist. Upstairs is a small chair, where the 4'11" woman would sit. It was Abraham Lincoln who commented on her diminutive stature, stating "So you're the little lady who started this big war?" Also intriguing is a drug box inscribed with her name that includes arsenic, used at the time to lighten a woman's complexion.

Orchard House, Concord, Massachusetts

When Little Women was first published in 1868, Louisa May Alcott was already in her mid-30s. Her autobiographical work living with her sisters was based in the **Orchard House**, which remarkably still stands today and was the backdrop for the latest movie release in 2019. Louisa's father, Bronson Alcott, a leader of the Transcendentalist movement, created the house by joining two early 18th-century homes already on the 12 acres of land he purchased in 1857. The family would live here from 1858 to 1877, a storied time for literature in Concord, where it also played host to Thoreau, Emerson, and Hawthorne.

House of Seven Gables, Salem, Massachusetts

A short walk down from the Salem waterfront will bring you to the birthplace of Nathaniel Hawthorne, **House of Seven Gables**. Built by Captain John Turner in 1668, this multi-chimney building was later occupied by a cousin of Hawthorne's who enjoyed telling young Nathaniel legends of the house and its inhabitants. The house holds six rooms of period furniture but the highlight for most is the narrow twisting staircase that leads to the second floor. Evidently, this secret passageway was used by an Abolitionist to hide slaves before their boat ride to Canada and freedom. Also on the grounds is a small red shanty where Nathaniel Hawthorne was born on July 4, 1804, and wonderful gardens that are the perfect place to have lunch and watch boats go in and out of the harbor.

Not Your Typical Walk in the Park, 3 Favorite Cemeteries

By the time I arrived at Mt. Auburn Cemetery just past 8 am, the parking lot was full and there were more than 100 bird watchers combing the grounds. Binoculars in tow, I passed under towering Norway maples, centuries-old cypress trees, and the resplendent purple-leaf beech tree, branches jutting wide in every direction. I strolled down the hillside and arrived on the shores of the Dell, a vernal pond straight out of a Victorian garden. Then I heard the first of many warbler songs that morning. Take a stroll in these cemeteries and they'll no doubt surprise you.

Mt. Auburn Cemetery, Watertown, Massachusetts

It might sound macabre to hike through a cemetery, but **Mt. Auburn** is no ordinary burial ground. Opened in 1831, it is the first large-scale designed landscape in the country. Now a National Historic Landmark, the 174-acre arboretum is known for its peaceful strolls along ponds or in dense woodlands which boast more than 700 types of trees. Walk amidst the century-old sugar maples while you visit the graves of Winslow Homer, Henry Wadsworth Longfellow, and Isabella Stewart Gardner. The Friends of Mount Auburn offer guided walking tours during the summer and fall. But the best time to visit is the first and second weeks of May, at the height of the warbler spring migration. Bring your binocs and a naturalist from Mass Audubon will help you spot the scruffy yellow chin of the northern parula warbler.

Forest Hills Cemetery, Jamaica Plain, Massachusetts

Enter the elaborate Gothic Revival gate at **Forest Hills Cemetery** and meander past a manicured green toward the hanging branches of a weeping birch tree and you don't see any graves. Forest Hills opened in 1848, stemming from the popularity of Mount Auburn. Joggers run on the wide streets, joined by bikers who are allowed to ride up and down the undulating hills. The bevy of activity continues around Lake Hibiscus, where families picnic and stare at the great blue herons standing on its stilt-like legs in the shallow water. Similar to the Forest Hills entranceway, there are no gravesites around the sprawling shores of the lake, so you quickly forget you're in a cemetery. At the annual Lantern Festival, visitors make paper lanterns and float them on the lake in remembrance of someone special. There are also classical music concerts and readings to commemorate the great poets and playwrights buried here, like EE Cummings, Anne Sexton, and Eugene O'Neill.

Granary Burying Ground, Boston, Massachusetts

Arguably one of the most popular sites on the Freedom Trail is the **Granary Burying Ground**, the final resting spot for Paul Revere, Samuel Adams, John Hancock, Peter Faneuil, all the victims of the Boston Massacre, and a Mother Goose, though historians are not positive if she is the Mother Goose. You can walk through the Granary in a matter of minutes, but you want to spend far longer discussing the heroic deeds these great men performed to grant us our freedom. Unlike other well-known cemeteries, there is no pomp surrounding the Granary, just layer after layer of short stubby headstones that reflect off the windows of a neighboring office building creating quite a juxtaposition.

A Stop to Antique Shop

Woodbury, Connecticut

With miles of handcrafted stone walls fronting classic Colonial homesteads, you really don't need too many excuses to visit Connecticut's Litchfield Hills. Yet, there is a special incentive to visit Woodbury in the southern tier, dubbed the "Antiques Capital of Connecticut." Whether you desire historic furniture, porcelain, rugs, paintings, books, mirrors, even sleighs and buggies, you'll find a dealer catering to your wishes at one of the more than 30 shops in town. An added bonus on weekends is the **Woodbury Antiques and Flea Market**, which runs every Saturday and Sunday from 7:30 am to 2:30 pm.

7 Unique Places to See Regional Theatre/Dance/Films

The Berkshires might take top billing as New England's summer cultural hub, but there are other locales worthy of your attention.

Williamstown Theatre Festival, Williamstown, Massachusetts

Home to the white colonnaded buildings and manicured lawns of Williams College, Williamstown becomes a peaceful respite for thespians in the summer months, when many of Broadway's top actors and directors relish the opportunity to be out of the stifling Manhattan heat. From the third week in June to the third week in August, the **Williamstown Theatre Festival** is one of the most renowned stages in the country for summerstock theater. Plays by some of the finest scribes of the 20th-century like Noel Coward, William Inge, Lillian Hellman, and Ben Hecht are performed in the new 550-seat MainStage Theater. There are also impromptu cabaret performances in area restaurants. Kevin Kline, Richard Dreyfuss, and Christopher Reeve are but a few of the many accomplished actors that performed here.

Colonial Theatre, Pittsfield, Massachusetts

It was September 28, 1903, when one of the gems of the gilded era, the **Colonial Theatre**, first opened to the public with the play, Robin Hood. Touring companies would appear weekly, bringing such stars at Ethel and John Barrymore, and Sarah Bernhardt, who performed in The Merchant of Venice. John Philip Sousa and the Ziegfeld Follies also entertained at the Colonial, which soon earned respect for its exceptional acoustics. Then the Depression came, and the theater fell on hard times, screening movies until 1949. Several years later it was sold and, for the next half a century, would be used as a retail store selling art supplies. Thankfully, the owner didn't tear down the old structure. In August 2006, after being completely rehabbed, the Colonial opened once again as a theater for plays, films, and concerts.

Jacob's Pillow, Becket, Massachusetts

Don't miss the chance to grab picnic food at the Becket General Store and head over to **Jacob's Pillow** for one of their free Inside/Out dance performances. Dancers from the School at Jacob's Pillow take the stage at 6:15 on Wednesday through Saturday nights for a 45-minute show. And what a stage it is—nothing more than a rectangular floor backed by maples and glorious views of the surrounding mountains. Then stay for the main event, which every summer usually includes the Mark Morris Dance Group.

Academy of Music Theatre, Northampton, Massachusetts

Built for $125,000 in 1890, the **Academy of Music** showed its first motion picture here eight years later. Harry Houdini, Mae West and a host of celebrities appeared on its stage, and scores of others graced its screen. Located in this college town, one of the oldest movie theaters in the country still boasts its original 19th-century balcony, lounge and private boxes.

Trinity Rep, Providence, Rhode Island

Since its founding in 1963, **Trinity Repertory Company** has been one of the most respected regional theaters in the country. The theater has produced 66 world premieres, mounted national and international tours, and, through its MFA program, trained hundreds of new actors and directors.

Goodspeed Opera House, East Haddam, Connecticut

Across a drawbridge that spans the Connecticut River sits the four-story gingerbread **Goodspeed Opera House**. Opened in 1877, the theater staged the original productions of Annie and Shenandoah and still delivers three musicals a year.

Ogunquit Playhouse, Ogunquit, Maine

Spend your day at the beach and then walk the scenic Marginal Way to Perkins Cove for the requisite lobster roll. Afterwards, wander over for a show at the **Ogunquit Playhouse**, one of the historic summerstock theaters in New England. Helen Hayes, Bette Davis, and Anthony Quinn have all graced the stage. To this day, the spacious building on a former farm is a blessed retreat for talented actors.

5 Special Spots to See a Musical Performance

Tanglewood, Lenox, Massachusetts

Five hundred glorious acres of manicured lawns and gardens, much of it overlooking Stockbridge Bowl (a lake), await the music lover at **Tanglewood**. It's no surprise that eastern urbanites flock to the Berkshires in the summer months to get their fill of culture here—it's so damn civilized. Listening to the Boston Symphony Orchestra perform Tchaikovsky on a cloudless night in August, one doesn't have to be a classical music aficionado to savor this spectacle.

Fenway Park, Boston, Massachusetts

One of the country's most celebrated baseball stadiums first opened in 1912. The acoustics might be so-so, but the chance to sing the words of every Billy Joel song along with thousands of others on the field is a thrill.

Shalin Liu Performance Center, Rockport, Massachusetts

Rockport is best known for Bearskin Neck and its collection of small boutique shops, ice cream stores, and restaurants that jut out into the harbor, ending at a rock jetty. Have dinner, take a stroll, and then head to the recently revamped **Shalin Liu Performance**

Center, a contemporary classical and jazz music venue whose floor-to-ceiling stage window overlooks the Atlantic.

Trapp Family Lodge, Stowe, Vermont
The Hills are Alive with the Sound of Music. If you have a chance to see a show at **Trapp's** meadow in summer, surrounded by the ridge of the Green Mountains and stars twinkling in the clear night sky, go! Grab yourself a pint of their award-winning Pilsner first.

Stone Mountain Arts Center, Brownfield, Maine
What happens when an acclaimed singer-songwriter grows weary of going on the road and wants to create a cultural arts center in her own rural community? In the case of Carol Noonan, she enlists the help of her husband Jeff Flagg and builds a timber frame barn in her backyard, the scenic foothills of the White Mountains in Brownfield, Maine (a 2 ½-hour drive from Boston, just over the New Hampshire line). Since its opening in August 2007, the **intimate 200-seat venue** has attracted bluegrass icon Ralph Stanley, country singer Marty Stuart, and Noonan herself, who former Globe music critic Steve Morse called "a deeply honest, soul-piercing singer."

4 Authentic Guided Day Trips

Authenticity is the buzzword in travel these days, the chance to live and feel like a local, not a tourist. Thankfully, there are many opportunities in New England where you have the chance to go beyond the boilerplate tours and get a real feel for the region while being led by an expert on the subject. These handful of day trips strive for genuine authenticity and hopefully reward you with lasting memories:

Bike to 5 Lighthouses in Portland with Summer Feet Cycling

Known for their weekend and weeklong bike trips throughout Maine, **Summer Feet Cycling** now offers a half-day guided bike tour to five lighthouses in the Portland area. Running daily from Memorial Day to October 31st, the 5-hour jaunt starts on a bike path alongside Willard Beach to Bug Light, which marks the entrance to the Portland Breakwater. From here, you'll cycle on to the Spring Point Lighthouse, the Portland Harbor Museum, and Fort Preble, a 19th century stone fort, before ending at the iconic Portland Head Light. You'll dine on sublime lobster rolls from a food truck while no doubt peering at the schooners that make their way in and out of Portland Harbor.

Drive the Dunes of Cape Cod with Art's Dune Tours

You must be doing something right if you're still in business since 1946. **Art's Dune Tours** is now run by Art Costa's son, Rob. Spend an hour in an air conditioned Suburban as you drive over the sand dunes on Provincetown's Cape Cod National Seashore learning about the unique topography as well as the long-standing dune houses that still cling precariously to the shoreline. One of the latest itineraries is a 3 ½-hour Land n' Lake Tour that mixes the dune drive with a paddle on saltwater out of East Harbor. Lunch will be served on a lake atop a raft.

Race a Genuine America's Cup 12-meter Yacht in Newport

One of the most unique opportunities in Newport is the chance to sail aboard an authentic America's Cup yacht that once raced in the actual competition. In **America's Cup Charters**' three-hour racing experience, you have the rare opportunity to step into Dennis Conner's soft-soled shoes. The boats include the Weatherly (1970 America's Cup winner), Nefertiti (1962 defender's trials), American Eagle (best known as Ted Turner's stepping stone to America's Cup victory) and Intrepid (the last classic wooden yacht to defend The Cup in 1967 and 1970). You could be chosen to be a primary grinder (grinding a winch as fast as possible so that the foresail can change direction), timekeeper, or handler of the mainsheet or rope.

Learn About the Ghosts and Goblins of Portsmouth

These days, it seems like every town in America has its requisite Ghost Walk, yet it helps to have a town with a lengthy history that warrants such investigation. The seacoast town of Portsmouth, home to one of the nation's best collections of Georgian and Federal architecture, including many homes still standing from the 1700s, seems ripe with intrigue. On a 90-minute nightly stroll into yesteryear, Roxie Zwicker, author of Haunted Portsmouth and now part of the tour company, **New England Curiosities**, thrills you with ghoulish tales, like that dastardly Phantom of the Music Hall. She also leads groups through the narrow streets to sites like the "Haunted Corner," where all 4 adjacent buildings have supposedly been home to uninvited after-dinner guests.

For the Family

10 Best Family Experiences

Kids come in all shapes and sizes, and, as we well know, strong likes and dislikes. There's the one boy who spends so much time reading about the Revolutionary War that you swear John Adams was his father. Meanwhile, his sister is busy building her volcano experiment on the back porch. The artistic child is content with a blank piece of paper and a lump of clay, as long as there's time to create. Fortunately, New England has fantastic sights to fit every type of child, and their parents too. After all, the apple doesn't fall far from the tree.

Museum of Science, Boston, Massachusetts

Budding scientists with a healthy dose of curiosity should spend a day at the **Museum of Science**. Children can experience the lightning show in the Thomson Theater of Electricity, say hello to the three-story-high T-red model, and dismantle computers all day long. Investigate! helps children think like scientists, developing questions, finding evidence, and drawing conclusions from such activities as exploring the human body. Or visit the solar system at the daily star shows offered at the Charles Hayden Planetarium.

Salem Witch Museum, Salem Massachusetts

Time to learn the sordid truths of Colonial mass hysteria. In **a huge room where life-size figures are lighted in sequence**, you'll hear from 9-year-old Elizabeth Parris, her cousin Abigail Williams, and a West Indian slave named Tituba who amused the girls and their friends during the long harsh winter of 1691 with tales of sorcery and witchcraft. Tituba was the first to be accused of witchcraft, but others in town quickly followed. When the leading cleric of the day, Cotton Mather, led the call for tolerance, the senseless killings finally stopped.

Mystic Seaport, Mystic, Connecticut

Stroll down Front Street, **a re-creation of a working whaling village** with all the requisite shops. In the cooperage, large casks are created to store the oil. A man sweats over a fire at the shipsmith, melding wrought-iron metal to create lances, harpoons, and spades to cut the blubber, while the printing press is busy advertising jobs for naive green hands, appealing to their patriotic side with a sign reading: "20 Proud Americans Wanted for the Good of the Country."

Be sure to visit the historic whaleboat, Charles W. Morgan, which recently underwent a $10 million restoration to make it seaworthy again.

Eric Carle Museum, Amherst, Massachusetts

It was 1995, when the acclaimed children's book author, Eric Carle, and his wife, Barbara, had a hankering to open up a small studio to showcase the artist's work on more than 70 books. Well, my friends, fairy tales do come true. **The Eric Carle Museum of Picture Book Art** opened on a far grander scale than even Carle could have imagined. Upon hearing about his neighbor's desire, Hampshire College granted the Carles their one wish and donated a 7.5-acre apple orchard on university grounds to build their museum. The 44,000-square foot structure houses the largest collection of children's book illustrations in America, including works from Carle's The Very Hungry Caterpillar, Maurice Sendak's Where the Wild Things Are and that mouse-loving artist, Leo Lionni.

Old Sturbridge Village, Sturbridge, Massachusetts

At New England's largest outdoor living history museum, **immerse your curious child in early 19th century American life** as you watch potters, shoemakers, tinners, and blacksmiths practice their crafts.

The Cape Cod League, Cape Cod, Massachusetts

Picnic on the grass, breathe in the briny sea, and then watch the game while your kids play pitch and catch behind the press box. Mo Vaughn, Albert Belle, and Frank Thomas all played ball in the 114-year-old **Cape Cod League**, which features the best college-age players (not technically the Minor Leagues) in summer.

Strawbery Banke, Portsmouth, New Hampshire

Back in its heyday in the mid-18th century, **Strawbery Banke** was the place for sailors and whalers to find a good pint of grog. Today, the collection of 40 antique buildings on 10 downtown acres showcases the lives of sea captains, wealthy merchants, and the working families who've called this plot of land on the Piscataqua River home. Check out the new Victorian Children's Garden, where kids can view carnivorous plants such as Venus fly traps and pitcher plants, observe hummingbirds and butterflies, and smell the herbs and flowers found in favorite perfumes, soaps, and colognes. There's also an opportunity to play period lawn games like croquet, a game the sailors of yore probably didn't play.

Story Land, Glen, New Hampshire

Story Land opened in 1954, a year before a man named Walt Disney would open his amusement park in southern California. Unlike Disneyland, **Story Land** still has a nostalgic, far more relaxed feel. Stroll Cinderella's castle, on premises since 1957, and then sample all 22 rides. Waiting lines are minimal, so you don't have to stress about not seeing the entire park in one day.

Mr. Bean, Freeport, Maine

Sixteen miles north of Portland is Freeport, Maine, the town where Leon Leonwood Bean opened a shop to sell equipment and provisions to hunters and fishermen over a century ago. Today, L.L. Bean's mammoth store is open 365 days a year, 24 hours a day, and sells almost any gear and clothing you would possibly need to enjoy Maine's great outdoors. **L.L. Bean for Kids** is located a half-block away, to ensure that your children stay toasty warm on those cool nights.

Owls Head Transportation Museum, Rockland, Maine

On the coast of Maine, just south of Rockland, stands **one of New England's finest collections of antique automobiles**, planes, and motorcycles. In the large exhibition hall, you'll find a 1901 Oldsmobile, World War I fighter planes, and an old Indian motorcycle. And they all still work! If you're lucky, you're in town during one of the days where they take guests on rides in their freshly polished Model T. That's a thrill for all ages.

5 Best Spots to See Wildlife

Want to see the Big Five in New England—Moose, Whales, Loons, Seals and Penguins (yes, at Mystic Aquarium)? With a little effort, you can make this a reality.

Time to Find Bullwinkle, Greenville, Maine

Stay at the **Lodge at Moosehead Lake** and then spend eight hours with your own private Registered Maine Guide. The trip leaves midday, and depending on the latest scouting, you'll hike and/or paddle to remote areas frequented by moose. It's also common to see white-tail deer, beavers at work building a dam, loons, ducks, fox, snowshoe hares, and possibly a bald eagle. Afterwards, you can relive the memorable day at a dinner prepared over an open fire or camp stove.

Loony over Loons at Gorman Chairback Lodge, Greenville, Maine

On the first morning after breakfast at **Gorman Chairback**, we met up with our guide, Katie. Katie leads day trips for the AMC's guests at the three lodges in Maine's North Woods, Gorman Chairback, Little Lyford, and the recently reopened Medawisla. We chose to canoe across 4-mile Long Pond with Katie and it was a wise choice. She shared the Old Town canoe with my wife, Lisa, while my son, Jake, and I grabbed the second canoe. We followed a family of loons, mergansers, and even spotted a bald eagle atop a dead hemlock tree. The waters of Long Pond were like glass that morning, reflecting the surrounding mountains atop the surface. All you could hear was that mesmerizing call of the loon as there was no other traffic on the pond. No boats, no canoes, nothing.

A Whale of a Good Time, Stellwagen Bank, Massachusetts

Hungry humpbacks, along with smaller minke whales, head to Stellwagen Bank from April to November to take huge gulps of fish that are attracted to this massive nutrient-rich mesa, 7 miles out to sea from Provincetown. Currents slam into the 18-mile-long bank, bringing nutrient rich cold water to the surface. This attracts fish, which in turn attracts numerous species of whales. The easiest access is from Provincetown, but there are also whaling tours leaving from Boston and Cape Ann.

Finding Harbor Seals on Monomoy National Wildlife Refuge, Cape Cod, Massachusetts

Both the Cape Cod Museum of Natural History and the Wellfleet Chapter of the Mass Audubon Society offer trips to North Monomoy Island in the summer to visit the National Wildlife Refuge. The seven-minute boat ride from Chatham drop you off on the shores of North Monomoy. Back in 1959, Monomoy was still part of the Cape, but a tumultuous storm and the constant battering of the waves severed this barrier beach from the mainland. Years later, more inclement weather split the island in two. You'll disembark and slowly make your way around the island to see the hundreds of harbor seals. The animals' playful heads bob up and down like lobster buoys.

Penguin Encounter, Mystic Aquarium, Mystic, Connecticut

There's no better welcoming committee to the **Mystic Aquarium** than those adorable beluga whales swimming in their outdoor pools just to the right of the entrance. Watch the trainers feed the whales, then walk nearby to see the large stellar sea lions. Afterwards, head inside to view the display of hypnotic jellyfish, including the graceful comb jellies and the long tentacles of the Pacific sea nettles, known for its painful sting. For an additional fee, you can have private time with a penguin in the Penguin Encounter. Pet his slick back feathers, watch him waddle around the small room, and see him dine on herring and squid as you learn about the diminishing habitat of the African penguins, now officially endangered.

4 Best Places
to Apple/Strawberry Pick

There's no better autumn outing than picking apples with family and friends, getting hot out-of-the-oven cinnamon doughnuts, washed down with fresh apple cider. Practically every rural town in New England has their favorite place to apple pick, but these are the ones we cherish:

Bolton Orchards, Bolton, Massachusetts

A rite of passage in our household. Head out on the Mass Pike east of Newton and 45 minutes later arrive at **Bolton Orchards** to apple pick for macs, macouns, honeycrisp, and other juicy New England varieties. Then grab our doughnuts, cider, and drive another 10 minutes to one of the finest corn mazes in the region, the **Davis Mega Maze**. There are more than 3 miles of paths through this complex maze, which has a different theme each year. Expect to spend hours finding your way out or begging the teenaged help for clues.

Russell Orchards, Ipswich, Massachusetts

Not far from the entrance to Crane Beach is **Russell Orchards** (143 Argilla Rd), a favorite stop for families since 1920. Stop in their store to find just-baked cider doughnuts, muffins, apple cider, hard cider, and fruit-flavored wine. Or head out into the fields to pick-your-own strawberries and apples. The annual strawberry harvest culminates with a Strawberry Festival in mid-June.

B. F. Clyde's, Mystic, Connecticut

On the outskirts of Mystic, **B.F. Clyde's** (129 North Stonington Road), first opened in 1881 and is home to the oldest steam powered cider mill in America. And what a contraption it is! Walk around the machinery, amazed that it still runs. Then hit the store to try the sweet cider, pumpkin bread, apple pies, and maple syrup.

Cold Hollow Cider Mill, Waterbury Center, Vermont

Several miles north of Ben & Jerry's on Route 100 is New England's largest producer of fresh apple cider, the **Cold Hollow Cider Mill**. Sample the goods and then stock up on other Vermont goodies like maple syrup, apple jellies, cheddar cheese, and honey mustards. There is no apple picking at this store.

6 Favorite Lodgings for Family Get-Togethers

Family resorts in New England are as varied as the region. Whether you crave the Mass or Maine coast, the mountains or lakes of Vermont, or a farm in New Hampshire, you'll find a spot for your family that's as comfortable as being at home...without having to do the dishes. Activities are just as diverse, like milking the cows with the whole gang, to going on a quiet beach stroll without the kids. Most important, the following six resorts passed the "Now What?" test with both our kids. Not once did they utter those words as they busily bounced from one event to the next.

The Winnetu, Martha's Vineyard, Massachusetts

When Gwenn and Mark Snider took the shell of an old motel and built this stylish Victorian resort of yesteryear, the island of Martha's Vineyard finally had the premier family resort it so desperately needed. **The Winnetu** is located four miles south of Edgartown, and a short walk to that glorious stretch of sand known as South Beach. Every one of the thirty-six suites, ranging from 1 to 4 bedrooms, features ocean views and a full kitchen, but the Sniders have done everything possible to keep the kids outdoors. Pee-wee tennis clinics start at 8 am. An hour later, children are whisked over to the clubhouse for morning activities like beach scavenger hunts or walks to Katama Airfield to watch the circa 1940 planes take flight. Afternoons are free for families to roam the island on a web of bike trails. You can pedal to the Vineyard's oldest settlement, Edgartown, and take the one-minute ferry ride over to Chappaquiddick. There you'll find miles of untrammeled beach at Cape Pogue Wildlife Refuge. Or venture another 6 miles past Edgartown to Oak Bluffs to ride the Flying Horses Carousel, the oldest operating carousel in the country, built in 1876.

Ocean Edge Resort, Brewster, Massachusetts
Driving along Route 6A in Cape Cod, it's hard to miss Boston banker Samuel Nickerson's turn-of-the-century Victorian mansion. Today, it's the centerpiece of the sprawling **Ocean Edge Resort**. While Mr. Nickerson's beachfront estate no longer houses the public, the resort more than makes up for it with over 400 guest rooms and townhouses. If you want to be close to the water, opt for one of the Bay Pine Villas where you're a short walk away from their private 700-foot expanse of beach on Cape Cod Bay. Add a golf course, six pools, bike paths that connect with the 26-mile Cape Cod Rail Trail, plus eleven tennis courts and you'll find it hard to bore Junior. The Ocean EdgeVenture Program also offers full and half-day programs for kids 4-15 if you need time by your lonesome to play those 18 holes.

Basin Harbor Club, Vergennes, Vermont
The kids are stand-up paddleboarding near the middle of the lake. My wife is sea kayaking with her

siblings and their spouses closer to the shoreline. Steady wind blowing through my hair, I'm at the tiller of an 18-foot sailboat accompanied by Granny Franny and her longtime beau, Saul. To celebrate a special birthday for Fran, my wife's extended family decided to book a week at the classic family retreat on the shores of Lake Champlain, the **Basin Harbor Club**. One glance at the lake from the Adirondack chairs perched on a bluff just outside the main dining room and you understand the allure. On the opposite shores are the steep rock cliffs called the Palisades and beyond that, the spine of New York's Adirondack Mountains. The Vermont side is not too shabby either, a bucolic blend of dairy farms, horse pastures, and their own requisite peaks, the Green Mountains. Come summer, this region is a warm embrace of emerald green fields and blue waters.

The beauty of this type of resort is that everyone, including the kids, has their independence. If Fran and my son Jake want to play a game of tennis, off they go. If Lisa's brother, Jeff, wants to throw a Frisbee with his son, Micah, after a competitive game of shuffleboard, go for it. We see each other at breakfast, sporadically throughout the day and then meet up for dinner. Yet, most afternoons, we find each other at the small beach, swimming over to the dock, and lounging on chaise lounge chairs with a pint of Vermont's Switchback Ale in one hand, book in the other. I can't resist the chance to bike every day. Any avid road biker will tell you that Addison Valley, Vermont, where Basin Harbor Club is located, is easily one of the top five biking destinations in North America. The backcountry roads have very little car traffic, great uphill climbs and downhill runs, and around every bend is another dairy farm, massive red barn, white church steeple, and glorious vistas of mountains and lake.

Tyler Place, Highland Springs, Vermont

Gone are those days of our youth at Camp Hiawatha when we would smack around the tetherball, dunk each other in the water, and swallow five roasted marshmallows whole. We're responsible adults now who have to set a good example for our youngins. But now and then it's healthy to lapse back into good ole childish play and what better place to do it than with our kids at a family camp. Set on grassy bluffs along the shores of Lake Champlain, **Tyler Place** is America's original family camp, opened in 1933. Families spend the afternoons together canoeing, swimming, fishing, what have you, while mornings and all meals are spent with your peers. Kids are split up into 8 different age groups and are led on a slew of activities that take advantage of Tyler Place's one-mile stretch of private shoreline on this massive lake. This leaves mom and dad to hike, bike, horseback ride, go on a naturalist-guided canoe trip, or simply lounge in a large Adirondack chair and listen to the waves lap ashore.

The Inn at East Hill Farm, Troy, New Hampshire

For suburban and urban families, there's no better way to relieve the stresses of modernity than to go back in time and spend a week at a farm. Parents give their kids a sense of exhilarating freedom and innocence that rarely exists nowadays. Set at the base of Mt. Monadnock in New Hampshire, the **Inn at East Hill Farm** fits that bill. Even the smallest tike can wander safely around the 150-acre resort, gathering eggs, milking the cows, and feeding the goats on this working farm. Counselors lead the children on scavenger hunts and arts and crafts projects throughout the day while parents can either participate or wander off and climb the 3,165-foot high Monadnock. Afterwards, cool off in the outdoor pool. Hardy meals like turkey with all the fixins is served family-style around large tables. Accommodations range from spacious guest rooms in the original 1830s inn to spanking clean two and three-bedroom cottages that dot the grounds.

Sebasco Harbor Resort, Sebasco Estates, Maine

As soon as you pull off Route 1 onto one of those Maine peninsulas that jut into the Atlantic like fingers on a glove, surrounded by the salty sea, you realize you're in for a treat. **Sebasco Harbor Resort** is perfectly set at the end of one of those peninsulas, overlooking the great expanse of ocean. The 600-acre retreat is truly a large playground for families, the reason why you meet people from all over North America who return to Sebasco year after year to get their dose of New England tranquility filled with delicious helpings of lobster and chowder. The view alone is worth the price of admission, looking out over the rocky shores past lobstermen in boats picking up their traps, to pine-studded islands and the wide open Atlantic. Yet, it's the family activities that truly separates Sebasco from the rest of the pack. Many hours are spent in the large saltwater swimming pool. Nearby, the kayaking center offers a number of guided paddles each day, led by a naturalist who will paddle you in the right direction to see harbor seals and ospreys.

From Monday to Friday, Camp Merritt will lead children 5 and up on daily excursions throughout the property. This includes creating tie-dyed shirts, heading to the ice cream stand for Moose Tracks or Maine Blueberry ice cream, and visiting the indoor Quarterdeck Recreation Center to go candlestick bowling and play pool, air hockey, and pinball. If you want to spend the day together, there are also a slew of options. Children can play golf with their parents on the 9-hole resort course or the 3-hole lake course, or take a lesson from the instructor at the Pro Shop. There are also tennis courts to practice your forehand. A pirate cruise is one of two boating choices. The other is a cruise to the many small villages surrounding the resort in Casco Bay, learning about the long history of lobstering and fishing in the region. At night, don't miss the campfire singalong and s'mores, a tradition at Sebasco.

5 Great Overnight Camps for Kids

More than just plain fun, parents should think of overnight camp as an education. Glance at the research done by the ACA (American Camp Association) and you'll realize that if your child spends a couple weeks at overnight camp, their growth in self-esteem, social skills, independence, physical and thinking skills, and sense of adventure is going to grow faster than if they were doing any other home-based activity. All you have to do is put in the time and energy to look for a good fit for your child. The following overnight camps have all provided an exceptional experience and lifelong memories for countless children:

Camp Schodack, Nassau, New York

Owner and director of **Camp Schodack** since 1970 (after taking over the reins from his father who founded the camp in 1957), Paul Krouner continues to add activities to his upstate New York property, like a go-kart track. There's water skiing, swimming, and kayaking on a nearby lake, and the usual baseball, basketball, and soccer. Yet it's the individual sports that gets the kids worked up, like a 300-yard zipline, high ropes course, batting cage, driving range, horseback riding, and rock climbing tower. Day trips to whitewater raft on the Deerfield River, visit The Baseball Hall of Fame, and backpack in the Adirondacks are just some of the many off-premises destinations. Though the camp is secular, that doesn't stop Krouner from offering tidbits of wisdom on values and morals at the weekly Friday night campfire talk.

Camp Keewaydin and Songaweedin, Salisbury, Vermont

For a camp to last over 100 years, they obviously have a recipe for success. In the case of **Keewaydin** and **Songadeewin**, it's a classic back to nature approach that stems from their stellar locale on the shores of Vermont's Lake Dunmore. Backed by Mt. Moosalamoo and the spine of the Green Mountains, kids have the option of canoeing, kayaking and sailing on the quiet lake or rock climbing or backpacking on terra firma. Or kick back near the rustic cabins and catch frogs in the lagoon, fish off the dock, or read a good book under the shade of a tall fir tree. Boys aged 16 and 17 can opt for a month-long paddling adventure in northern Quebec led by Cree Indian guides.

Camp Kebeyun, Alton Bay, New Hampshire

Nestled on the shores of Lake Winnipesaukee, parents love the locale of the all-boys camp, **Kabeyun**. Kids love the flexibility. Founded by John Porter in 1924, their motto is "You can choose to do anything you want, but you can't choose to do nothing." Each day (except Sunday), boys get to select their own activities, so if you want to get that sailing license or hook a large lake trout, go for it. There's also waterskiing, windsurfing, wakeboarding, canoeing, swimming, archery, a ropes course, and a top-notch tennis program. Basketball and soccer games are also on the agenda, but Kabeyun strives for a non-competitive, laid-back atmosphere. Out-of-camp adventures can last from one to six days and include backpacking through the Whites.

Camp Walt Whitman, Piermont, New Hampshire

Maybe it's the 2:1 camper to staff ratio or the nurturing environment that stresses the importance of being a responsible member of a community and how to be a good friend. Perhaps it's the appealing location on the shores of a placid lake nestled in the White Mountains or that large heated pool they use when the lake waters get too cool. Whatever the reason, it obviously works since **Camp Walt Whitman** enjoys an annual camper return rate of 85 to 90 percent. Turning 73 in 2021, Walt Whitman features a laundry list of attractions including 11 tennis courts, a driving range, batting cage, gymnastics, pottery, and the requisite water sports of sailing, kayaking, windsurfing, and waterskiing.

Camp O-AT-K, Sebago, Maine

In 1906, Reverend Ernest Joseph Dennen, an Episcopalian minister from Lynn, purchased a farmstead on the shores of Lake Sebago, Maine, to give 20 boys the unique opportunity to become part of a character-building program he called the Order of Sir Galahad. Today, 270 boys from more than 30 states and 12 countries descend on this large lake every summer to learn those same leadership skills at **O-AT-KA**. This being Maine, campers also have the opportunity to build their own graphite fly rod, grasp the age old art of fly-tying and, at the age of 14, learn the necessary outdoor living skills (map and compass reading, building a fire and shelter) to become certified Junior Maine Guides.

For the Downhome Foodie

6 Favorite Lobster/Clam Shacks

Talk about lobster rolls with a Mainer and you enter into a territorial catfight where everyone seems to choose their local favorite. I'll avoid that right now and simply say these are the places my family returns to as often as possible:

The Lobster Shack at Two Lights, Cape Elizabeth, Maine

If you're yearning to find the best lobster roll with sea view, then it's hard to top the **Lobster Shack** in Cape Elizabeth. Not far from where Winslow Homer set up shop on Prouts Neck, this lobster-in-the-rough joint overlooks that same boulder-strewn coastline Homer loved to paint. Order your food at the window of the rustic shack, wait for your number to be called, and grab a picnic table that rewards you with vistas of the Atlantic as it pours into Casco Bay and is framed by two lighthouses. They've been serving lobster on this salty spit of land since the 1920s, but it wasn't until 1969 that the Lobster Shack made its debut. Three generations of the same family have been running the show ever since, the latest being Katie and Jeff Porch. Every day in summer they make the 20-minute drive to Portland Pier and purchase their daily allotment of some 200 lobsters. The shrimp, crabs and clams are also bought close by, securing their freshness and sustaining the local economy.

McLoons Lobster, South Thomaston, Maine

This red shack is **a must-stop in mid-coast Maine**. Choose either mayo or hot butter on the bun and then get ready for the freshest lobster meat you've tasted in a long time. Just writing this is making my mouth water.

Beal's Lobster Pier, Southwest Harbor, Maine

If you spent the day hiking in Acadia National Park, then you've earned your fill of lobster at the seafood-in-the-rough **Beal's** in the small fishing village of Southwest Harbor. Grab a picnic table overlooking the lobstermen and dig into the red crustacean, lobster rolls, and clam chowder. Toddler-friendly fare includes grilled cheese sandwiches and French fries.

Arnold's Lobster and Clam Bar, Eastham, Massachusetts

Grab a tray at almost any hour from late morning to closing time at **Arnold's** and more than likely you'll be standing in a line, waiting for lobster rolls and a mound of tender onion rings to bring to nearby Coast Guard Beach, or for a fried clams or lobster dinner devoured at the outdoor picnic tables under the pines. The owner, Nick Nickerson, equates his success with the unyielding desire to find the tastiest seafood around, and if he has to pay extra to the local fishermen, so be it. Scallops that have been collected by fishermen in Cape Cod Bay arrive by 10 am. He prefers to get his clams for steamers at the Town Cove on the Eastham/Orleans border. Clams for frying can come as far away as Rhode Island, but Nickerson prefers the ones that come from sand beds instead of mud flats, stating that the latter tastes like, well, mud. For lobster, he prefers the hard shelled version found on the back shore of the Cape, off Coast Guard and Nauset Beaches. Work off your meal by playing a round of miniature golf next door.

Woodman's, Essex, Massachusetts

Hungry after a day of swimming at nearby Wingaersheek or Crane Beach, we always seem to end up at **Woodman's** for an early dinner. People queue up to order lobsters of every size imaginable, buckets of tender steamed Ipswich clams, fried shrimp, corn on the cob, and mounds of onion rings. The signature dish, however, is the fried clam platter. Conventional wisdom has it that the fried clam was invented at Woodman's on July 3, 1916. Lawrence Dexter "Chubby" Woodman was frying potato chips for the Fourth of July celebration when someone suggested that he drop a few steamers into the hot fat. The rest is mouth-watering history. To this day, Woodman's is still run by members of the Woodman clan. You can sit down at one of the picnic tables inside the restaurant or better yet, head outside and have dinner on the edge of the Essex River Basin. The pencil thin legs of the blue heron can often be found lurking deep in the beds of these estuarian mud flats searching for his own bucket of clams.

The Clam Box, Ipswich, Massachusetts

Open in 1938, **The Clam Box** (246 High St) is one of those iconic road trip stops you dream about. Order your heaping plate of fried clams, scallops, and shrimp and grab a seat at one of the outdoor picnic tables. Then take a bite of the sweet meat, lightly battered, and you'll understand why it deserves all the hype.

5 Unique Food Outings

The Maine Windjammer Lobster Bake, Penobscot Bay, Maine

A day of salty air and pulling on ropes can build up an appetite. Fortunately, the Maine Windjammer sailing fleet is known for their hearty meals. And if you're expecting Navy grub, you'll be surprised to know that Windjammer food is so cherished that no less than three of the boats have already published their own cookbooks. The Captains source local harvested ingredients and often provide their own produce from home, like flowers, syrup, honey and eggs. Fresh baked breads are cooked in a cast-iron wood stove, with stews and salads another staple of the seafaring diet. The highlight of every trip, however, is the all-you-can-eat lobster bake, served with steamers and corn. **Captain Barry King of the Schooner Mary Day** once had one young man eat 13 lobsters in one sitting. Talk about getting your money's worth! Captains know this is the signature meal on the cruise so they strategize carefully, taking the weather into consideration, finding the best beach for dining, arranging to pick up fresh lobster at the last minute from a local. The side dishes include corn on the cob, steamed clams, salad, potatoes, and often linguica. Hot dogs and hamburgers are also available for those foolish souls who don't like lobster. Dessert is usually served back aboard the schooner. Expect hot pie topped with schooner-cranked ice cream or something more gourmet like butterscotch-topped gingerbread with sautéed apples. Then someone usually pulls out a guitar and banjo and you sing sea shanties under the brilliant night sky. The only way to digest!

Ben & Jerry's Factory, Waterbury Center, Vermont

Get the scoop on the whole ice-cream making process from cow to carton at the **Ben & Jerry's factory** in Waterbury, Vermont. A short slide show tells how Ben and Jerry completed a $5 correspondence course from Penn State University on ice-cream making to become manufacturers of America's number one ice-cream flavor—chocolate chip cookie dough.

Then take a behind the scenes tour of the plant and watch workers churn out ice-cream to the beat of rock-and-roll music. If each one of the employees on the tour seems happy, they should be. Every Ben & Jerry's worker goes home with three free pints of ice cream a day! Visitors get to sample each of the ice creams being made that day and decide whether the New York Super Fudge Chunk has enough chunks in each scoop to pass inspection. People on the tour can also suggest new ice cream flavors and names.

A Visit to The Grafton Village Cheese Company, Grafton, Vermont

The Grafton Village Cheese Company receives 6,000 gallons of butter milk from Vermont's Jersey cows every day to create their award-winning cheddar cheese. Watch the short video on how see the cheese is hand made as you peer through the glass window to see the workers in process. Then strut over to the gift shop to sample the wares. Their 6-year old Stonehouse is the oldest cheddar made in the state, while the 2-year-old Classic Reserve Cheddar is still the most popular. Also be on the lookout for a traditional farmhouse cheese.

Portuguese Fare in New Bedford, Massachusetts

New Bedford is home to the country's largest Portuguese population. Venture down Acushnet Street and you'll see the mom-and-pop joints dishing out the spicy stews, many with olives, beans, linguica (pork sausage) or cacoila (marinated roast pork). Arguably the best restaurant for Portuguese food in New Bedford is **Antonio's** on Coggeshall Street. Start with the kale soup and then it's on to the national dish, bacalhau (salted cod), baked, broiled in casseroles, or eaten in a sandwich. Remember that those exciting spices you're tasting inspired celebrity chef Emeril Lagasse. A native of nearby Fall River, Emeril's mother is Portuguese.

Massachusetts Historic Hole-in-the-Wall Joints

Finally, there's those dining spots you won't find in any Massachusetts guidebook. Ones like the pint-sized **Agawam Diner in Rowley**, a joint that's been keeping the natives sated with lamb shank, chile, and double-layer banana nut cake since 1954. How about **Bub's BBQ** on Route 116 in Sunderland, where the pulled pork and ribs could rival the barbeque shacks in Memphis. At the original **Kelly's Roast Beef** in

Revere, crowds line up on a sunny day to grab their Dagwoodesque roast beef sandwich and head across the street to eat on the beach. **Four Seas** in Centerville, on Cape Cod, has been keeping kids happy since 1934, scooping up ice cream within the nautical decor. **Mielke Confections** in Great Barrington has been dipping the local produce—strawberries and apples—in their milk and bittersweet chocolate since 1961. The White Hut in West Springfield is known for burgers topped with a heaping mound of caramelized onions. These are the real finds, the ones locals venture to but rarely discuss with out-of-towners for fear of standing in a longer line.

10 Best Places for Pizza

If you think Bostonians are the only people loyal to their beloved pizzerias, head to other parts of New England. You can start with New Haven where every local is passionate and will vehemently defend their favorite pizza locale, often generation after generation. Then move on to Rhode Island, central Massachusetts, Vermont, New Hampshire, and Maine, where the pizza wars can be more contentious than finding the best lobster roll in the state. We offer these ten picks simply as a starting point.

Frank Pepe Pizzeria Napoletana, New Haven, Connecticut

The thin, slightly charred crust on **Frank Pepe**'s pizzas are so incredibly tasty that my children plead with me to get off the highway every time I roll past New Haven. It was Frank Pepe who started the "apizza" craze in New Haven, when his Neapolitan dialect couldn't get around the word, pizza. In 1925, he installed his first coal-powered oven and the rest, as they say, is history. If you think Lawrence "Chubby" Woodman transformed the clam-eating industry by dropping a clam into a frying vat, try one bite of Pepe's white clam pizzas. The tender morsels are dripping with clam juice, with the perfect mix of salty sea, grated parmesan cheese, olive oil, and oregano. Or choose my kids' favorite, the original tomato pie topped with mozzarella, garlic, and basil.

Sally's Apizza, New Haven, Connecticut

The nerve of Salvatore Consiglio, nephew of Frank Pepe, leaving the family business to start his own apizzeria in 1938. In the same Wooster Square neighborhood, no less. When he died in 1989, more than 2500 people came to his wake and funeral, including Connecticut senators and many devoted Yale University graduates. Doonesbury creator Garry Trudeau sketched **Sally's** restaurant in his early strips when he was a student at Yale, probably as a way of killing time while waiting in line. Lines are practically a guarantee, but don't let your impatient friends sway you into going to another pizza joint. For a thin crust tomato pie, also cooked in a coal-powered oven, this is about as close to perfection as it gets, especially in summer when the tomatoes are fresh and the juices commingle happily with the oily crust. I don't live in New Haven so thankfully I don't have to take sides between Pepe's and Sally's. I love them both.

Modern Apizza, New Haven, Connecticut

Open in 1934, **Modern** has the same lengthy history of Frank Pepe's and Sally's, but since it's not located on Wooster Street, never gets the same out-of-town crowds. Head inside where you have views of the historic brick oven and get ready to dive into another splendid pie. Like Pepe's, Modern does the white clam pizza right. If you want to spice it up, go with a clams casino, adding bacon and peppers.

The smooth thin crust at Modern has more strength than Pepe's or Sally's, so it's a good place to top it off with meats, like a personal favorite, bacon, onion, and hot cherry peppers.

Caserta Pizzeria, Providence, Rhode Island

Located on Federal Hill, several blocks from Atwells Avenue, **Caserta's** has been serving Providence's preferred pies for over 50 years. Judging from the line that always snakes around the tables on the black-and-white tile floor, they should hit the century mark in stride. The crust is so good at Caserta's, a chewy mix of dough and tomato sauce, that cheese is optional. Give the plain pie a chance, topped with a heaping amount of mushrooms and onions, and you'll realize that cheese isn't a necessary staple to savor this tasty treat. In fact, Caserta's is so cherished that you'll find many people on line asking for them not to cut the pie so that they can freeze it and save it for another day. Also sample the "Pig in the Blanket," sausage doused in tomato sauce and rolled in dough that would be a huge hit at Fenway Park.

Al Forno, Providence, Rhode Island

In 1980, Johanne Killeen and George Germon, owners of **Al Forno** restaurant, placed a sheet of raw pizza dough onto the searing grates of their charcoal grill. Little did they know they would create a grilled pizza phenomenon that lasts to this day. Come to Al Forno and order one of the grilled pizza appetizers. The thin dough, charred from the grates, tastes like Indian naan bread. Yet, when paired with extra virgin olive oil, pomodoro tomatoes, a thin layer of cheese, fresh herbs, and toppings like roasted eggplant and corn, you have a one-of-a-kind pizza that will whet your appetite for another exceptional meal at this renowned restaurant.

Enrico's Pizza, Fiskdale, Massachusetts

Close to Old Sturbridge Village, **Enrico's** is a favorite with families, who come for the brick oven pizzas, spicy wings, and good selection of salads. Specialty pies include the scampi, a thin-crust white pizza topped with grated parmesan cheese, grilled shrimp, roasted garlic, and mushrooms. For meat lovers, there's the panciuto, a more traditional tomato and mozzarella sauce coated with sausage and pepperoni. The pizzas are served on top of old tomato sauce cans, a nice touch.

Santarpio's, East Boston, Massachusetts

A fixture in East Boston since 1903 and part of a tradition for most airline travelers flying in and out of nearby Logan, **Santarpio's** is still family-owned and operated. Known for their minimalistic decor, their barbecued lamb and sausage, and of course, their thin-crust pizza that will take you back to the best pizza joints in Naples.

Pizza on Earth, Charlotte, Vermont

Every Friday night, you can follow the stream of cars that make their way some 13 miles south of Burlington to the farming community of Charlotte. They come to a small cottage on a farm, surrounded by rolling hills, to order the pies that come piping hot out of the 800-degree wood-fired oven. **Pizza on Earth** is an apt name for a pizzeria that takes full advantage of its setting, using ripe vegetables that were plucked that day from the neighboring farms. So if it's eggplant season, expect roasted eggplant smothered on the thin crust pizza. When it's time to gather the zucchinis, Pizza on Earth creates a curried zucchini pizza topped with feta cheese. This is agrarian pizza at its best, especially when you venture here in summer and early fall during the height of the harvest.

Flatbread, North Conway, New Hampshire

Started in Amesbury in 1998, the **Flatbread Company** now owns 16 pizzerias from Maui to Whistler to Somerville. Yet, it's their locale in North Conway that has the Granite State all abuzz. Maybe it's the Zen-like ambiance with all those Tibetan designs and the massive wood-fired clay oven plopped down in the center of the room. But I happen to think it's the Coevolution, topped with roasted red peppers, red onions, olives, goat cheese, garlic, and mozzarella. Much of the produce is from local organic farms and you can taste the difference.

Otto Pizza, Portland, Maine

Let's hear it for the slice shop, the old-time pizzeria where you can duck in for lunch, dinner, or in the wee hours of the morning, order a slice, mosey over to the counter and woof it down in record time. They seemed to be going the way of the typewriter and video stores until **Otto** opened in 2009 and instantly received adulation from ravenous Mainers. Walk into the small shop on Congress Street, not far from the Portland Museum of Art, and grab whatever pie just came out of the oven. It's all good, from the crunchy crust on the oversized slice, to the blend of mozzarella, romano, asiago, and fontina cheeses, to the unique combinations of toppings like the yummy bacon, scallion, and mashed potato pie. The white bean, roasted tomato, herb, and red flake pie is another winner that no doubt will have you venturing to this small space more often than your personal trainer would like. C'mon, it's only a slice!

3 Great Locales for Craft Beer Lovers

It's no surprise that some of the best craft beer in the world can be enjoyed right here in New England. The website RateBeer released its list of the Top 100 Brewers in the World for 2019, and three of the top-five breweries are in our region. Vermont's Hill Farmstead remains the world's best, followed by two Massachusetts breweries: Boston's own Trillium lands at No. 3, and Tree House Brewing Company is the fourth-best brewery. Then there's Heady Topper, brewed by The Alchemist in Stowe, Vermont, often voted the best-made beer in the world. To get your fill, head to these special spots:

Stowe, Vermont
Now that the **Alchemist** moved from Waterbury to a larger facility in Stowe, the town has evolved into a craft brew hub. Sample Heady Topper along with other local favorite IPA's like Focal Banger and Hellbrook at their state-of-the-art Visitors Center opened in July 2016. Then make your way up the hill to Trapp Family Lodge. Best known as the family that inspired the classic movie musical, The Sound of Music, the von Trapp's turned to Austrian-style lager in 2015, reaping accolades like Silver Medalist at the Great International Beer Festival since its debut. Tour the brewery, one of the largest in the state, and

then taste the award-winning Bohemian Pilsner, amber Vienna Style Lager, and the ultra-smooth Golden Helles at the new **Trapp Brewing Bierhall Restaurant**, best paired with a plate of bratwurst.

Metrowest Boston

With the surge in popularity in craft brew this past decade, it's no surprise that **City Brew Tours** has also grown substantially, now offering tours in 11 cities, including Boston. Their guided 5-hour ($99 per person) Original Boston Brew Tour makes 4 stops at some of the finest breweries in town, like Slum Brew, Dorchester Brewing, and Down the Road. But I'm a huge fan of what's happening in the Boston burbs, especially those dreamy IPAs created down the road at the **Trillium brewery in Canton**, and, of course, the much-hyped **Tree House**, 45 minutes away in Charlton. Lately, however, I've been happily consuming **Exhibit "A" beers**, especially their IPA, Cat's Meow, and their delicious German Kölsch-style beer, Goody Two Shoes. Glad to see that Exhibit "A" and their brewery in the original Jack's Abby home in Framingham is one of the 4 breweries folks visit on the MetroWest Boston Tour offered by City Brew. You'll also get a chance to try another local favorite, Cloud Candy IPA, created by the **Waltham brewery, Mighty Squirrel**. It's a great way to spend the day, including lunch, letting someone else drive while you sample the wares.

Portland, Maine

One taste of my first **Bissell Brothers** brew at **Pai Men Miyake** in Portland and I was smitten. That citrusy New England IPA appeal, with just the right amount of hoppiness, perfectly washed down my tasty ramen. Every time I stop in Portland, I now make a pitstop at one of the local breweries, whether it's outside at the picnic tables at **Rising Tide** or that burgeoning foodie destination of Washington Street to try one of the **Oxbow** sours. The list of local microbrews continues to expand, so even these three choices could be obsolete in a decade.

Best Farm-Next-To-Table Dining Experience

Primo, Rockland, Maine

There are farm-to-table restaurants and then there are farm-next-to-table restaurants. **Primo** sits on four-and-a-half acres of rolling farmland, and by all means take a stroll of the grounds before sitting down for dinner at the charming two-story abode. James Beard Award-winning chef, Melissa Kelly, is both the head of the agricultural operations as well as the talented chef at the helm. Start with the surprisingly tasty snap peas, sprinkled with sea salt, and then dive into the thick-cut pork chops, accompanied by sweet roasted brussels sprouts. The casual top-floor lounge serves house-made charcuterie, pizzas, and oysters.

All the Lodging Choices You'll Need

Top 12 Country Inns to Get Pampered

Not too long ago, a bed and breakfast was simply an extra room in someone's house to rent out. You ate family style, shared the bathroom, and had little or no privacy. Times have changed. B&Bs have evolved into country inns that cater to the whims of couples with the finest services available, from high thread count linens on stuffed king-size beds to whirlpools with rainforest showers that soak every inch of your skin, to spa treatments that rejuvenate overstressed bodies. Then there's the lure of New England, with its pick of ocean, mountain, or countryside view. Here are our favorites:

The Mayflower Inn, Washington, Connecticut

When art dealer Robert Mnuchin and his entrepreneurial wife Adriana bought the dilapidated **Mayflower Inn** in 1992, the couple finally had a place to store all those French, English, and American antiques they had purchased on their travels. Indeed, they spared no expense furnishing their 25 rooms with four-poster beds, rugs from Tabriz, linens by Frette, and, of course, mahogany wainscoting in the spacious marble bathroom. You'll feel like lord of the manor at this sumptuous escape, especially when you stroll the 28-acre grounds, landscaped exquisitely with rhododendrons, stone walls, even a running stream. Listen to the church bells ring from the nearby green and you'll quickly realize the village of Washington has changed little since the time of George.

Cliffside Inn, Newport, Rhode Island

All it takes is a short stroll from the **Cliffside Inn** to understand its allure. Within minutes, you'll access Newport's famed Cliff Walk, a 3 ½-mile long gem of a trail perched above the Atlantic offering views of the sloping lawns and backsides of those summer "cottages" the Vanderbilts, Whitneys, and Astors built at the turn of last century. But first you have to leave the cozy confines of this circa-1876 Victorian home. Each of the 13 guest rooms and 3 suites is distinctive, like the Garden Suite, a duplex with your own private garden, a double Jacuzzi the size of a small swimming pool, two fireplaces in the bathroom and bedroom, six dimmers to control the lighting, and Peruvian limestone tiles that are heated so your tootsies won't get cold between that long walk from bath to bed. If you're looking for a specific room, you'll have to book well in advance. The earliest requests usually come from brides who want a special room for their wedding night.

The Inn at Castle Hill, Ipswich, Massachusetts

Few inns in America can look out from their wraparound porch onto miles of uninterrupted salt marsh and beach and call it their own. Then again, few inns are owned by land conservation groups like the Trustees of Reservations. In 1949, the descendants of plumbing magnate Richard Crane bestowed their entire 2100-acre estate in Ipswich to the Trustees. This includes their 59-room Stuart-style mansion, the grounds designed by none other than the Olmsted brothers, the more than 4 mile stretch of Atlantic beach, and a ten-room 19th century cottage and tavern which was renovated in 2000 and is now called the **Inn at Castle Hill**. Breakfast, included in the price, uses the eggs and milk farmed down the road at the Trustees' 1000-acre Appleton Farms. Afterwards, walk a loop through the mix of marsh, dunes, and beach and you'll no doubt be smitten.

Blue, Plum Island, Massachusetts

If you yearn for pounding surf and a long stretch of sand to walk barefoot for hours, then it's hard to think of a better beachfront locale in New England than **Blue** on Plum Island. This 13-room inn is smack dab on the beach, next door to the coastline and marsh of Parker River Wildlife Refuge. Accommodations include 5 stand-alone cottages with full kitchen, hot tub, and fire pit, ideal for a family escape. Or grab another couple and all the fixings for a classic New England lobster bake, and reserve the 2-bedroom Blue Suite. The 2200 square-foot space offers a full kitchen, private hot tub, fireplace, and your own private entrance to the beach, which you probably won't leave until the sun rises the next morning.

Salt House Inn, Provincetown, Massachusetts

Upon arrival at the **Salt House Inn**, you're handed a map of Provincetown designed by owners David

Bowd and Kevin O'Shea. It pinpoints favorite restaurants (which, of course, were reserved by David and Kevin weeks before your arrival), off-the-beaten-track beach strolls, the best market to pack a picnic, and eclectic stores like the one that sells vintage housewares. Details, after all, are what separate goodness from greatness, and fortunately Bowd and O'Shea have the necessary experience in the hospitality world to know exactly what their clientele clamor for, preferably comfort with a nourishing, yet not-in-your-face dose of service. The 15-room property, originally cottages for salt mine workers in the 1850s, is on a quiet road, a stone's throw from the hustle and bustle of Commercial Street. A rarity in Provincetown, the inn comes with parking lot and also offers a second floor sun terrace to relax in one of the rocking chairs. Breakfast is a high point, where O'Shea is happily back cooking scones, an egg dish like frittata or quiche, ham and cheese croissants, and offering a Vermont yogurt station with toppings like granola and jam.

Union Street Inn, Nantucket, Massachusetts

The sole reason why the **Union Street Inn** receives rave reviews from guests and national press? Expertise. Ken Withrow was the manager of Ian Schrager's Royalton Hotel in Manhattan. Wife Deb's background is in retail management at Henry Bendel and Fiorucci. She's also a talented chef as you'll soon find out at the gluttonous breakfast, which more than likely features their signature dish, challah French toast topped with blueberries and/or strawberries and only served with Vermont maple syrup. Less than a 5-minute walk from the ferry, near the restaurants and shops on cobblestone Main Street, Union Street Inn offers only 12 rooms, the reason why it's a challenge to book in the summer months.

The Guest House at Field Farm, Williamstown, Massachusetts

From outside, the **Guest House at Field Farm** in Williamstown is nondescript if not downright ugly. Then you enter the Bauhaus-era home, now a 5-bedroom inn run by the Trustees, and you understand the brilliance of American modernism. All those rectilinear lines created the perfect opportunity to place large glass windows around the exterior and take in the stunning views of Mount Greylock. Walking into the living room is like walking into a post-modern early 60s museum set where Don Draper is your host. Unlike the architecture, all furniture seems to have curves from the Isamu Noguchi glass coffee table to the swan-backed couch by Vladimir Kagan. For visitors hoping to take in the art at the Clark Art Museum, there's no better setting.

Grafton Inn, Grafton, Vermont

Very few places in New England epitomize small town splendor and charm better than the historic hamlet of Grafton, Vermont. In the mid-1800s, Grafton had approximately 1,500 people and 10,000 sheep. Wool was turned into cloth, local soapstone quarries were used to create stoves, sinks, and foot warmers. By the end of the century, **Grafton's inn** known as the Old

Tavern had played host to such luminaries as Ralph Waldo Emerson, Henry David Thoreau, Rudyard Kipling, Ullyses S. Grant, and Teddy Roosevelt. However, the village soon took a turn for the worst. Sheep farmers moved west to find new land, and the mills shut down in search of cheaper labor farther south. By the end of the Depression, the population was less than 100 and most of the houses were up for sale. If it wasn't for the generosity of Pauline Dean Fiske, and the foresight of her nephews, Dean Mathey and Matthew Hall, the historic homes would have been torn down and turned to pasture. With their aunt's money, the two nephews founded the Windham Foundation in 1963 and proceeded to restore the entire town, including the Old Tavern. The turnaround was dramatic. The village now looks like it did a century and a half ago, replete with requisite white steeple, sparkling white clapboard homes, and a country store. Yet, this is no Disneyesque version of a Currier & Ives painting, but a working town where locals mix with Windham Foundation workers and a growing number of second home buyers.

The Pitcher Inn, Waitsfield, Vermont
Each of the 11 rooms in **this Relais & Chateaux property** has a distinct Vermont feel. The large Mallard Room evokes the image of duck hunting. Decoys line the wooden trim of the bed and wainscoting resembles the look of a marsh. In the Trout Room, birch trees were used to create the bed frame, a fly-fishing desk is fully stocked, and a semi-circular verandah overlooks a rambling stream. More than forty local

craftspeople were hired to give the rooms this classic agrarian appeal. Local farms also supply the food for a memorable meal.

Chebeague Island Inn, Chebeague Island, Maine

Impeccably restored in 2004, **Chebeague Island Inn**, perched above the shores of Casco Bay's largest island, never seemed to catch on with mainlanders. That was until Mainer Casey Prentice and his family purchased the circa-1920 estate and instilled the property with a much needed dose of youthful enthusiasm. Word spread quickly about the dining scene and how they create tasty dishes from local catch. Now Portlanders think nothing of taking the 15-minute water taxi or ferry to Chebeague for cocktails on the wraparound porch, dinner, even an overnight stay in one of the 21 rooms found in the three-story home. Overnight guests have the option of sea kayaking or lobstering with locals.

Grey Havens Inn, Georgetown, Maine

Plant yourself in an Adirondack-style rocking chair on the verandah of the **Grey Havens** and wait for the fog to lift. You'll soon be able to spot the lobstermen cruising from buoy to buoy to pick up the day's catch, and the occasional harbor seal popping his head out of the water to see what all the fuss is about. Built in 1904, this turreted, gray-shingled home and its mellow pine paneling is conducive to lounging, especially on this perfect perch above the Atlantic. Request an oceanside room and while away the day with novel in tow. Close by, Reid State Park has trails along the rugged shores and through the inland forest where dwarf pines have felt the brunt of forceful winter gales. Another must-stop is the Georgetown Fishermen's Coop. Lobsters are fresh off the boat, cooked with steamers and corn on the cob.

Saltair Inn, Bar Harbor, Maine

One look at that long lawn that sloping down to the sea at the **Saltair Inn** and you immediately know you made a wise choice. It only gets better when you realize that the location of the inn is located on the quiet side of West Street, within easy walking distance of the restaurants and shops of Bar Harbor, but far away from the crowds. Owners Matt and Kristi are the perfect team. Kristi serves up yummy breakfasts each morning like blueberry pancakes and stuffed french toast, while Matt divulges the insider information on Bar Harbor and Acadia National Park that only a local would know. He'll design a great bike loop on the Carriage Path Trails, or tell you about a small trail near the restrooms at the Bass Harbor Lighthouse that leads down the freshly cut stairs to a bed of rocks, where you not only have great views of the lighthouse, but can spot dolphins and seals in the sea.

7 Best Resorts Along the Sea

Just thinking about a family getaway along the Atlantic coast and you start to breathe a bit easier. Surrounded by beach, ocean, and the salty air, New England's finest coastal resorts are therapeutic retreats. There's no better place to leave the stresses of everyday life behind and relax in a gorgeous outdoor setting. Try these 7 ocean resorts for starters:

Ocean House, Watch Hill, Rhode Island

Built in 1868, the Victorian-style **Ocean House** sits on 11 acres of land including some prime beachfront real estate. In its heyday, the hotel offered 159 rooms and was once used as a set for American Aristocracy, a 1916 silent film starring Douglas Fairbanks. In 2003, damage from the salty air finally took its toll on the grand hotel, and it shuttered for a short time. The following year, plans were drawn to re-create Ocean House in an even more sybaritic fashion, decreasing the number of rooms and suites to 64, creating an on-site spa, and still including croquet with a croquet pro, no less.

Wequassett Resort, Harwich, Massachusetts

I firmly believe that the most memorable resorts have more than just a sumptuous room, stellar restaurant, and sublime stretch of property. They have a distinct personality that usually stems from the owners.

Mark Novota, co-owner of the **Wequassett Resort** since 1977, has that genuine joie de vivre. He's obviously enjoying his life and he wants his guests to join in on his sheer exuberance. So it's not enough to simply have the top restaurant on the Cape. He wants his guests to wander over to the café afterwards to dance their booty off to a live band. It's not enough to have a large heated pool, surrounded by cabanas and oversized chaise lounge chairs. No, he'll have one of his captains escort you by motor boat to a deserted beach on the Cape Cod National Seashore, passing the countless gray seals that call the Pleasant Bay waters home. Still not convinced? You can have your own private clambake for family and friends in one of those poolside cabanas overlooking the Pleasant Bay shoreline as the sun sets. A shuttle takes you over to the quaint shops and restaurants in Rockwellesque town of Chatham. There are bikes at your disposal to ride the nearby Cape Cod Rail Trail, through the cranberry bogs that turn beet red in autumn. The har-tru tennis courts are now lit at night and there's easy access to one of the region's finest private golf courses, the Cape Cod National Golf Club. And the grounds are brimming over with every type of Cape flower imaginable, from hydrangeas to azaleas to colorful day lilies.

Chatham Bars Inn, Chatham, Massachusetts

There's something aesthetically pleasing about a pool that's built on the same level as the ocean waters that surround it. That's exactly the case at the curving **Chatham Bars Inn** pool that overlooks the sailboats of Pleasant Bay at the elbow of the Cape. While the kids play around the fountains, mom and dad can take a long swim underwater and listen to classical music that's pumped in through the pool speakers. A nearby circular bar serves lemonade and far more tropical drinks. And, of course, you may have as many of those fluffy white towels as deemed necessary. But there's much more than the pool at this favorite family getaway. Cruise on their fleet of boats to see the whales or go fishing, or stay on land with a round of tennis, golf, or a five-star treatment at the spa. Open year round, Chatham Bars Inn has an intriguing calendar of events such as wellness weekends, wine classes, mixology classes, clambakes, oyster roasts, kids programming, and an art series. Chatham Bars serves organic New England cuisine sourced locally from the Chatham Bars Inn Farm at its restaurants on site: Stars, The Sacred Cod, The Beach House, and The Veranda.

The Wauwinet, Nantucket, Massachusetts

Flanked by Nantucket Bay and the Atlantic Ocean in a less congested section of Nantucket, the **Wauwinet** combines historical charm with the natural sea-scape of Melville's favorite island. Open the French doors to your balcony, breathe in the salty air, and admire the landscaped gardens. After a few bottles of bubbly, you might think you spotted Moby Dick swimming alongside the boats in the harbor. If you're feeling active, the resort has windsurfing rigs, sunfishes, mountain bikes, and tennis facilities, including two clay courts, all available to guests.

You also can go four-wheeling on the beach to the remote Great Point Lighthouse, or grab a bike and pedal six miles on the Polpis bike path to the village of 'Sconset, where rose-trellised cottages with names like "The Snuggery" and "Very Snug" line the narrow streets. Nearby 'Sconset Beach, on the eastern end of the island, seems like the right place to indulge in a bit of seaside romance.

Inn by the Sea, Crescent Beach, Maine

With its prime location overlooking Crescent Beach in Cape Elizabeth, Maine, near the photogenic Portland Head Light, **Inn by the Sea** could have easily stayed the status quo and guests would still return year after year. Instead, they poured millions of dollars into renovations, updating the rooms and adding fantastic 2-bedroom suites, building a cozy bar, a glass-enclosed restaurant with requisite ocean views, full-service spa, and all the green trimmings one would hope in an eco-resort. Rooms are cleaned with non-toxic Green Seal product, the fitness room has recycled rubber floors, and the pool is heated with solar panels. This conscientious attitude also stems to Sea Glass restaurant, which does its best to serve indigenous fare from the surrounding farms and sea, like Maine foraged mushroom tarts or steamed wild Maine mussels. Dog lovers will be happy to know that the restaurant is not only dog-friendly, but serves a doggie menu on the outdoor deck that includes Angus steak tips, a doggie cookie, and ice cream.

Cliff House, Cape Neddick, Maine

Technically speaking, the **Cliff House** is not a new build. But after closing for a year and spending upwards of $40 million, the newly revamped Cliff House has little in common with its predecessor. Now that Phase II of the construction is complete, adding additional rooms and an adults-only infinity swimming pool, it will gain its rightful place as one of New England's finest resorts. To truly appreciate the resort's name, stroll on the hotel grounds down by the tidal pools and peer back at the wall of rock that houses the lodging atop a precarious cliff. Located in Cape Neddick, on the outskirts of Ogunquit, it's one of the most dramatic vistas of the Maine coastline. The 2-story lobby and all rooms have blue carpeting, a nautical theme, and premium oceanfront locale with mesmerizing views of the flat sea leading to the horizon. On premises, there's a 9,000 square-foot luxury spa, infinity pool and hot tub, indoor lap pool, casual lobster-in-the-rough restaurant called Nubb's, and the more upscale Tiller restaurant, where you can dine on freshly caught lobster overlooking the jagged shoreline. There's also the opportunity to play 18 holes of golf at the adjacent golf course or venture out on guided kayaking, horseback riding, mountain bike riding, and lobstering excursions. Needless to say, the kids won't get bored here.

The Samoset, Rockport, Maine

The crown jewel of Maine's mid-coast, the 230-acre **Samoset Resort** in Rockland, recently undergone extensive room renovations. All 178 rooms and suites now have a contemporary coastal flair, thanks to the blue and white palette that livens up the décor. Samoset has also debuted six new Family Suites which include a kid's bunkbed room, separate from the main bedroom, ideally suited for families with tweens and teens. The bunk room offers amenities like board and video games and fun, educational books about Maine. The resort also features an 18-hole golf course, outdoor and indoor heated pools, hot tubs, tennis courts, health club, spa, basketball courts, and fire pits. Also nearby is my favorite breakwater to walk in the state and the James Beard-award winning restaurant, Primo.

4 Resorts in the Countryside

Ahh, breathe in those firs and spruces and fill up those lungs up with fresh air.

Omni Mount Washington Resort, Bretton Woods, New Hampshire

Eyes widen and mouths gape as soon as you turn off New Hampshire's Route 302 and witness your first glimpse of the **Mount Washington Hotel**. The amazement builds on the one-mile driveway up to this immense six-story white edifice, created in an era when grand hotels were as common as one-room schoolhouses in the Whites. It's a multi-tiered wedding cake topped with scarlet frosting and ringed by those broad shouldered revelers known as the Presidential Range.

Dinner and breakfast are served in the octagonal main dining room, which has seating for a mere 730 people. A four-course meal amply feeds adults while kids are treated to their own children's menu. Between bites of grilled cheese sandwiches and chicken nuggets, the young ones whisk their parents onto the dance floor, accompanied by live music. 27 holes of golf, 12 tennis courts, horseback riding, hiking, fishing, and biking are a sampling of the summer activities.

Woodstock Inn, Woodstock, Vermont

First opened in 1793 as the Richardson Tavern, the 146-room **Woodstock Inn** now caters to families who want to take advantage of the surrounding pastoral setting. From the steps of this grand, Colonial-style resort, it's only a 25-minute walk to the peak of Mt. Peg. The inn also rents bikes to ride on Vermont's lightly traveled backcountry roads. Travel north on Route 12 and you'll pass meadows so green and fertile, you'll want to jump off your bike and plunge your hands in the soil. Back at the Woodstock Inn, there's a Robert Trent Jones, Sr., designed golf course, a heated outdoor pool, ten outdoor tennis courts, badminton, horseshoes, volleyball, and a large indoor sports center where parents can soak their tired bodies in Jacuzzis. The latest addition is the unveiling of the Red Barns, renovated rustic barns down the road from the property that showcase the wealth of produce already growing at the surrounding Kelly Way Gardens. Certified organic by the Vermont Organic Farmers Association, the gardens boast more than 200 varieties of produce including 55 varieties of tomatoes, 75 berries and orchard plantings, 50 herbs and edible flowers, a mushroom glen, annual and perennial flowers, honey, and hops. Taking advantage of this bountiful harvest, the Red Barns offer cooking demonstrations and a dining facility in their Red Barn Dinner Series.

Twin Farms, Barnard, Vermont

This 300-acre estate was once author Sinclair Lewis's wedding present to his wife and the setting for their outlandish house parties. The lodgings are all-inclusive, so all meals and activities are included in the rates. Stay in one of the ten cottages surrounding the farmhouse, barn and main inn. Everywhere you look are glorious views of Vermont mountains, valleys with wildflowers or colorful leaves depending on the season, stone walls and covered bridges. Known for their excellent food and top notch wine cellar, **Twin Farms** will not disappoint even the most discerning of foodies. All kinds of recreation are offered, from hiking, biking, fishing, golf, horseback riding in the warmer months, to ice skating and skiing on their private hill in winter.

The Equinox Resort, Manchester Village, Vermont

Presiding over a Colonial green that evokes images of a Currier and Ives greeting card, Manchester Village, Vermont is one of those quintessential New England villages where one strolls between shops, golfs, and goes off-road driving. That's right. Land Rover opened its first year-round 4X4 driving school in America at **The Equinox**. Spend an hour or longer with one of the Equinox's expert instructors on an all-natural circuit. The sinuous route climbs the slopes of 3,816-foot Mt. Equinox, weaving through thick woods and scratching brush, over rocks, ruts, and streams to compress a lifetime of off-road experience into a one-mile route. Once a fashionable summer retreat for affluent northeasterners and American Presidents, the 240 year-old Equinox continues to captivate guests who yearn for the elegance of yesteryear coupled with a bevy of modern-day amenities. Other activities include fly-fishing with an Orvis guide or sampling one of the best golf courses in the state. Afterwards, rest your weary muscles in the newly refurbished spa. Many of their treatments use products native to Vermont, including maple sugar, wildflowers and mineral clay.

7 Great Boutique Hotels

Searching for a smaller property, one with a sense of style or located in a stellar location. Look no further:

Winvian Farm, Morris, Connecticut

It was 2006 when the Smith family decided to transform their 113-acre estate in Litchfield Hills into one of New England's most unique and exclusive resorts called **Winvian**. They hired 15 architects to create "cottages" nestled into the meadows, ponds, and rolling farmland that flanks their circa-1775 Main House. Today, these 18 finished works are rare architectural gems where inside each spacious abode, you'll find hidden wonders like a fully restored 1968 helicopter that now serves as the bar and entertainment center in the Helicopter Cottage; or The Treehouse Cottage, a two-story structure 32 feet off the ground, suspended atop a tree. When not admiring the cottages, you can stroll through the wildflowers to a pond where great blue herons take flight or opt for a much longer hike in the surrounding White Memorial Foundation, a 4,000-acre wildlife sanctuary. Afterwards, treat yourself to a massage at the spa or a swim in the pool. Winvian is also a Relais & Chateaux property as you'll soon realize at dinner, a 4-course feast.

Spicer Mansion, Mystic, Connecticut

Perched on a hill overlooking the Mystic town spires and waters of Long Island Sound, the former summer home of Captain Elihu Spicer had fell into disrepair and was scheduled for demolition. Thanks to the Gates family of nearby Stonington, the estate was purchased, restored to its 1853 grandeur, and is now an **8-room Relais & Chateau property**. Enter this gem of a building and saunter into the Rose or Blue Salon and you'll immediately be wowed by the ceiling frescoes, inlaid wooden floors, original moldings, and doors so tall that the Jolly Green Giant could enter. Service at this inn is impeccable from the innkeeper to the bellhop, but the highlight is the six-course prix-fixe meal that starts in the salon with canapés and cocktails and ends in the intimate dining room. Talented chefs take the best locally sourced seafood and meats and places it artistically on Bernardaud china, guaranteed to seduce all senses. Paired with wines served in Baccarat crystal, be thankful that you can plop down in that king-sized bed just up the stairs.

Weekapaug Inn, Weekapaug, Rhode Island

Originally built in 1899, the **Weekapaug Inn** was destroyed in a hurricane in 1938. That didn't stop owner Frederick Buffum from rebuilding the inn the very next season on the same 1 ½-mile stretch of undeveloped Rhode Island beachfront. Today, this old-fashioned resort—no phones or televisions here—is still run by the Buffum family. The Weekapaug sits at the end of a tidal pond whose shallow waters are ideal for young swimmers. There are twice-daily organized programs for children, like nature hikes and sandcastle building. They also feature tennis, sailing, canoeing, shuffleboard, and, befitting a century-old inn, croquet.

Ale House Inn, Portsmouth, New Hampshire

With an up-and-coming food scene, including several chefs nominated for the prestigious James Beard Award, and one of the nation's best collections of Georgian and Federal architecture, Portsmouth has become a popular weekend getaway come summer or fall. The problem is the lack of available lodging near the center of town so you can easily walk to that collection of 40 antique buildings at Strawbery Banke and the boutique shops, restaurants, and microbreweries near the waterfront. That's the reason why the 10 rooms of the **Ale House Inn**, located on the 3rd floor of a circa-1880 building, are always in high demand. One of the first Lark Hotels properties to debut (they also manage the Hotel Portsmouth on the other end of town), the Ale House Inn has the look of a cruise ship hallway. Plop your bags down in the light-filled rooms and grab your complimentary growler. Then make your way over to the Portsmouth Brewery for a taste of one of their signature brews, the Surrender to the Flow IPA. That will whet your appetite for the selection of New Hampshire oysters, harissa-rubbed grilled shrimp, and fries cooked in duckfat found at The Franklin. Work off dinner with a stroll across Memorial Bridge into Maine.

Beachmere Inn, Ogunquit, Maine

There are three reasons why the **Beachmere Inn** continues to sell out summer after summer—location, location, and location. Perfectly situated on the lower portion of Shore Road, a small gate at the far end of the Beachmere's sprawling lawn opens onto to the mile-long cliff walk they call the Marginal Way. Head downhill and you can stroll to the main beach, stores and restaurants in Ogunquit. Far more breathtaking vistas are to the right of the gate as you peer out at the jagged coastline and vast Atlantic. Soon you're in the compact neighborhood called Perkins Cove, where you can shop for painted lobster buoys and grab your requisite lobster roll at Barnacle Billy's.

250 Main, Rockland, Maine

Don't let the non-descript, almost minimalist exterior of **250 Main** fool you. Inside the welcoming and spacious lobby, you'll find local art on the walls, the latest copy of Art New England on coffee tables, and comfortable contemporary furniture where you can savor that complimentary glass of wine at happy hour. Opened May 2016, the 26-room boutique hotel appeals to art lovers who can walk over to nearby Farnsworth Art Museum and the new Center for Maine Contemporary Art. Rooms also come with the latest modern accoutrements like heated towel rack, heated floors, rainforest shower heads, and a sumptuous mattress destined to emit a sigh. If you can make it out of bed in the morning, head up to the rooftop terrace for glorious views of the Atlantic and all those ferries heading out to the mid-coast Maine islands.

West Street Hotel, Bar Harbor, Maine

After days of hiking, biking, and sea kayaking in Acadia National Park, there's arguably no better place to unwind than the welcoming **West Street Hotel** in Bar Harbor. Take in the mesmerizing seascape from your balcony, overlooking Bar Island and Sheep Porcupine Island and all the boats docked in between. Or head to the rooftop pool for an energizing dip. You also have the option to swim at the Bar Harbor Club across the street. Their Olympic-sized pool is situated right on the edge of the ocean overlooking the expanse of sea and mountains. The property is within easy walking distance to all the restaurants in town. So sample the zesty grilled fish tacos at Side Street Cafe, the blueberry pancakes at 2 Cats, and the heavenly black raspberry ice cream at Ben & Bills Chocolate Emporium.

Have Tent, Will Travel, 10 Places to Camp

Whether you crave mountains, lakes, rivers, or ocean, the variety of New England terrain is best appreciated when you can slow down and spend several nights in its sweet embrace. Make the decision to camp, then throw the alarm clock away and wake up to the sounds of loons echoing across a lake. At night, after the s'mores have been devoured, stare at the clear sky and shimmering stars. Without the distraction of a television or computer, you'll get to know your kids again. Here are 10 of my favorite places to spend the night under the skies of New England:

Lake Waramaug State Park, New Preston, Connecticut

For those of you who think the beauty of Connecticut is nestled along the shores of the Long Island Sound or on the banks of the Connecticut River (the town of Essex comes to mind), we bring you Lake Waramaug. Tucked away in the Litchfield Hills, surrounded by small rounded peaks, this is one of the most cherished campgrounds in the state. The 78 sites are located in a forest near the waters of this majestic lake. Go swimming at the beach, fish for largemouth and smallmouth bass, or grab the canoe in the early morning hours for a quiet paddle before the kids are up.

Charlestown Breachway, Rhode Island

Charlestown Breachway is one of those coveted Little Rhody gems that I'm not too happy to give away. The long strip of sand is not yet covered with beach towels and ocean temperatures touched by the Gulf Stream can reach a downright balmy 70 degrees. But the real reason I love Charlestown is that you can also swim and paddle at the state's largest coastal pond, Ninigret, a short walk away. Other activities include surfcasting for stripers, windsurfing on the pond, and walking on the trails of Ninigret National Wildlife Refuge. The 75 camping sites are on the east side of the Breachway.

Mount Greylock State Reservation, Adams, Massachusetts

If you crave fresh mountain air, it's hard to top these 15 sites near the summit of Massachusetts' tallest peak, Greylock. Look up and you see scenic Stony Ledge, where the rocky cliffs offer magnificent views of Greylock's summit. Yet, even more mesmerizing is the v-shaped wedge of trees that form a valley between the peaks known as The Hopper. However, you'll have to earn these primitive campsites, since they're hike-in only. The easiest way to the campground is to take the more gradual 1.3-mile trek from the parking area on Rockwell Road. Hardcore hikers can try the 2.4-mile uphill climb from Williamstown. Once you've set up the tent, trails branch off in every direction to keep you occupied during the day.

Nickerson State Park, Brewster, Massachusetts

Located near the elbow of Cape Cod, the 420 well-spaced camping sites at Nickerson State Park are in extremely high demand during the summer. If you're one of the fortunate few to snag one, have fun exploring the hiking and biking trails that snake along the ponds and through the woods, including the 25-mile-long Cape Cod Rail Trail. Nickerson also features three of the Cape's 300-plus kettle ponds, filled with fresh water, so you can rent a canoe and paddle the serene waters of Cliff, Little Cliff, and Flax Ponds.

Boston Harbor Islands, Boston, Massachusetts

First stop for most visitors to the Boston Harbor Islands is Georges Island, reached via a 45-minute ferry ride from Boston's Long Wharf. Georges is the home of Fort Warren, built in 1833 and used during the Civil War as a training ground for Union Troops and prison camp for more than 2,000 Confederate soldiers, including the Vice President of the Confederacy, Alexander Stephens. From Georges, you can board a smaller ferry toward Grape Island, where history is replaced by uninterrupted nature. This is an ideal spot for walking on grassy paths past fields of wild roses, under towering birches, collecting blackberries and raspberries, and spending a night or two at the small campground. Overnight camping is also available on neighboring Lovell (popular for its outer beach) and Bumpkin Islands. Each island holds 10 to 12 sites.

Button Bay State Park, Addison, Vermont

Bike through Addison and you'll realize you're smack dab in the middle of sublime pastoral scenery. Head north on Button Bay Road and to your right are glimpses of stacked hay, lounging cows, rows of corn ready to be reaped, tall silos, and the spine of the Green Mountains. On your left are the waters of Lake Champlain, with the Adirondack Mountains rising from the opposite shores. This is the setting for Button Bay State Park. Located on a bluff along the southern shores of Lake Champlain, all of the 72 sites here have exceptional views of the Adirondacks across the water. Swim, canoe, bike, or talk to the resident naturalist at the nature center.

Lafayette Campground, Franconia Notch State Park, New Hampshire

When it comes to stellar mountain location, Lafayette Campground, located at the base of Franconia Notch, fits the bill. Snag one of the 97 sites, spaced evenly in the woods and along a creek, and you'll be at one of the finest starting points for outdoor activity in the White Mountains. You can choose to swim in nearby Echo Lake, bike on trails to Cannon Mountain, or take some of the best hikes in New England to Lonesome Lake, Basin-Cascades, or the ridge walk atop Mt. Lafayette.

Hermit Island Campground, Phippsburg, Maine

There are numerous campsites found along the Atlantic shoreline, but to actually reserve a campsite with an ocean view is a rarity. Yet, some of the 275 sites at Hermit Island Campground can stake this claim, overlooking the waters of Casco Bay. Hermit Island is a 255-acre peninsula in Small Point at the southern tip of Phippsburg. You can choose to grab a site along the sandy beach, atop the rocky cliffs, near the tidal pools, or in the forest. Then hit the water to fish, sail, paddle, and swim. The campground also owns a 50-foot deep-sea fishing boat that sails daily for cod and tuna.

Blackwoods and Seawall Campgrounds, Acadia National Park, Maine

Situated in a forest of spruce and shrubs, Blackwood's 306 sites are conveniently located on the east side of Mt. Desert Island. Near the crowded Park Loop, the sites tend to fill up faster than Seawall, located on the island's quieter west side. Seawall's 214 campsites are nestled in the woods, near self-guided nature trails and a short walk to the tidal pools that hug the Atlantic shoreline. Once situated at either campground, you're in close proximity to mountain biking on the 43 miles of carriage path trails, canoeing on Long Pond, and climbing Cadillac, Champlain, and Acadia Mountains for those exquisite views of the islands in Frenchman Bay.

Baxter State Park, Millinocket, Maine

The 246 campsites at Baxter, set in the North Woods of Maine, are spread out over 10 campgrounds. Some are accessible by road, others are hike-in only backcountry sites. Russell and Chimney Pond, near the base of Katahdin, are extremely popular. Not surprisingly, these sites fill up fast. Kidney Pond and Daicey Pond offer rustic cabins with beds, gas lanterns, table, chairs, and firewood. Outside of climbing Katahdin, there are 178 miles of trails, including the last ten miles of the Appalachian Trail, over 200 miles of streams, and numerous fishing holes to catch trout and find moose wading in the shallow waters.

3 Favorite AMC Huts

It was 1876 when 39 outdoor lovers met in Boston and formed an organization devoted to the exploration of the White Mountains. Several in the group had visited Europe and saw firsthand the Alpine huts, mountain refuges provided to shelter hikers. They were determined to bring this type of lodging overseas for the growing ranks of hearty "trampers," as hikers were called at the time. A dozen years later, their ambitions came to fruition with the opening of the stone Madison Spring cabin, set between the 5,000-foot peaks of Mount Madison and Mount Adams in the White's Presidential Range. Cost was fifty cents a night, and since the backpack was yet to be invented, hikers slung their food and clothing in a blanket tied shoulder to hip.

Three more huts, furnished with stoves, were built to accommodate the steady stream of climbers. Yet, it wasn't until 1922, when a young iconoclast named Joe Dodge was hired as Pinkham Notch hutmaster, that the AMC as we know it, began to take shape. A tireless devotee of the mountains, Dodge was cherished by his employees for his work ethic and honesty. When he retired in 1959, he left a chain of seven backcountry huts that stretched over 50 miles, each cabin a day's hike away from the next. After Supreme Court Justice William O. Douglas reaped accolades on the region in a 35-page spread in National Geographic in 1961, the AMC would have to build an eighth and final hut, Mizpah Spring, to lodge the latest batch of outdoorsmen.

In 2003, the AMC hut system expanded to Maine, where they would save 4 historic sporting camps in Maine's famed 100-Mile Wilderness section. These are the huts I find most appealing:

Lakes of the Clouds Hut, White Mountains, New Hampshire

Conditions need to be ideal to walk the historic Crawford Path through the Presidential Range. Once you venture beyond Mizpah Springs Hut to Mount Pierce, you're above treeline on a ridge walk, entirely exposed to the weather since there's really nowhere to hide. In decent weather, you'll be treated to the views of the bald knob atop Mount Eisenhower while walking in a lunar-like landscape. Bordered by velvety green sedge and moss, you'll find alpine wildflowers in bloom like bog laurel, white bunchberry, and purple fireweed. Then you spot the **Lakes of the Clouds hut** and its lofty perch atop a 5200-foot ridge with stunning vistas of Mount Washington Hotel below and the Cog Railroad ambling slowly up to the Mount Washington summit. Spend the twilight hours looking at the glorious view and then peering at the twinkling stars above (no light pollution here). The next morning, after a filling breakfast, climb on the hardscrabble rock the last 1.4 miles to the summit of Mount Washington, New England's tallest peak.

Galehead Hut, White Mountains, New Hampshire

Like most of the trails in the White Mountains, the Gale River Trail begins with forgiving dirt and mud, quickly changing to unforgiving rock. For most of the 4.6-mile climb, you'll be serenaded with the sounds of rapids rushing down the nearby river. Crossing over the waterway countless times on rock and log bridges, smelling the fragrant pine, the last bit is a steep ascent on awkward slabs of rock. No doubt tired, you'll make it to your oasis for the night, the **Galehead Hut**, where a sign outside the door simply reads: "Built 1932, Elevation 3800 feet." Plop down on the long bench outside the lodge and admire the panorama of peaks. Ridge after ridge, a carpet of green falling down the flanks to the valley below, like peering at a Japanese silkscreen in Technicolor. Don't be in a rush to leave.

Little Lyford Lodge, 100-Mile Wilderness, Maine

Opened in 1873 as a timber camp for those tough-as-bark men who chopped down trees and then rode atop the logs on rapid-churning rivers to the paper mill, **Little Lyford** made the transition to a sporting camp at the turn of last century. "Sports" as they would call them, would take the long train ride from Boston and New York to fish for native brook trout on the waters of the West Branch of the Pleasant River and hunt deer. In the past two decades, however, many of these rustic retreats, nestled deep in the woods across much of northern New England, have closed up and vanished because of declining business. Many have become private homes, never to be open to the public again. Little Lyford was headed in that unfortunate direction when the Appalachian Mountain Club made the bold move in 2003 to acquire Little Lyford and three other historic sporting camps in Maine's famed 100-Mile Wilderness section. People can now hike, canoe, or cross-country ski on a 60-mile corridor of pristine wilderness backed by the mountains of the Appalachian Trail and laced with hidden ponds and rivers that are populated with far more moose than humans.

At Little Lyford, seven cottages are nestled in a velvety green grove, surrounded by the tall pines and birches of the northern forest. Thankfully, the lodging has been updated since the days of lumbermen, but each cabin still has a rustic appeal with woodstoves and propane lanterns, along with heating and hot showers. Meals are still served family-style in the main lodge and you'll want a good hardy dinner after spending your day outdoors. A short walk brings you to Little Lyford Pond, a majestic gem backed by the peaks of Baker and Indian Mountains. Other trails lead to the West Branch of the Pleasant River, a tumbling stream teeming with brook trout, and Gulf Hagas, dubbed "the Grand Canyon of Maine," where the same river plunges through a narrow canyon, creating waterfalls and swimming holes.

Favorite Maine Huts & Trails Hut

12 years after Poplar Springs Hut was first built in Carrabassett Valley, the nonprofit group, Maine Huts & Trails, is making good on its lofty goal to build 12 eco-lodges in the Maine wilderness. There are now four huts in the system across a 45-mile span. Work on the next hut is expected to start in approximately two years. A consortium of big-name players such as L.L. Bean, New Balance (who runs two factories in Maine), and the Sugarloaf Ski Area are now financial supporters. And the Carrabassett Valley New England Mountain Biking Association (NEMBA) is using the latest round of funding to create some of the finest singletrack trails in New England. Yes, you can choose to hike or mountain bike hut-to-hut.

Stratton Brook Hut

As soon as you leave the car behind and start hiking or mountain biking the Stratton Brook Trailhead, you'll smell the sweet balsam and follow the butterflies as they fly from goldenrod to goldenrod. Climb gradually under the tall pines on Newton's Revenge Trail and some 90 minutes later you'll arrive at the **Stratton Brook Hut**. And what a beauty it is, all light wood with an interior that rewards with floor to ceiling windows overlooking the 4,000-plus foot mountains of the Bigelow Range. We had a private room, the opportunity to shower, and a chance to down a Maine microbrew or glass of wine to toast your achievement. We strolled up to the Vista, where a lonely bench looked out on a wide swath of uninterrupted wilderness including that stupendous view of the Bigelow Range and its mighty backbone that forms a ridge walk on the Appalachian Trail. A blanket of green formed a carpet on the flanks of the peaks, leading to ribbons of blue, where rivers carved through the valley. Not a bad place for Happy Hour!

About the Author

Steve Jermanok is the author of **Outside Magazine's Adventure Guide to New England** and **New England Seacoast Adventures**. He's also penned chapters for Frommer's, Lonely Planet, and Discovery Travel guidebooks. He has written more than 600 stories on New England for The Boston Globe, Yankee, Boston Magazine, Boston Herald, AMC Outdoors, and numerous other publications. In 2003, a film he co-wrote with brother Jim, **Passionada**, was released in over 80 theaters nationwide by Samuel Goldwyn Films. It was primarily filmed in New Bedford and South Dartmouth, Massachusetts. In 2012, he created **ActiveTravels**, a membership-based boutique travel agency with wife, Lisa Leavitt, that has sent clients on authentic travel experiences across the globe, including creating detailed itineraries for those venturing to New England. He resides in Newton, Massachusetts, with his wife, Lisa, two children, Jake and Melanie, and a favorite white buffalo stuffed animal.

You can get in touch with Steve at
https://activetravels.com
or emailing **steve@activetravels.com**
Follow on Facebook or Instagram: **@activetravels**

Regional Index

Northern Maine

8 Summer Drives That Will Keep You Smiling
The Maine Moose Run, Rangeley to Kingfield, Maine,
Page 23

10 Most Instagrammable Sites
Peering Down at Somes Sounds from Atop Acadia
Mountain, Acadia National Park, Page 32

10 Classic New England Hikes
Gulf Hagas, Brownville Junction, Page 55
Mount Katahdin, Baxter State Park, Page 56

10 Ways to Enjoy Acadia National Park
Bike the Carriage Path Trails, Page 86
Sea Kayak Frenchman Bay, Page 87
Hike Acadia Mountain, Page 88
Sail a Friendship Sloop, Page 88
Bike Schoodic Peninsula, Page 89
Rock Climb Otter Cliffs, Page 90
Hop Aboard Diver Ed, Page 90
Walk the Ocean Path, Page 91
Popovers at Jordan Pond Gatehouse, Page 92
Lobster Rolls at Beal's or Thurston's, Page 92

5 Great Fall Foliage Activities Away from the Crowds
Canoe the Allagash River, Page 93
Hike the Bubbles, Acadia National Park, Page 94

5 Special Spots to Bird Watch
Machias Seal Island, Off of Cutler, Page 100

5 Places to Canoe or Kayak
The Maine Waterways with Mahoosuc Guide Service,
Page 105

5 Places to White Water Raft/Kayak
Kennebec River, The Forks, Page 108
Penobscot River, Millinocket, Page 109
Dead River, Eustis, Page 109

6 Winter Adventures
Cross-Country Ski Hut-to-Hut in Carrabassett Valley,
Page 140
Two Nation Snowmobile Vacation, Presque Isle,
Page 138

5 Best Spots to See Wildlife
Time to Find Bullwinkle, Greenville, Page 188
Loony over Loons at Gorman Chairback Lodge,
Greenville, Page 188

6 Favorite Lobster/Clam Shacks
Beal's Lobster Pier, Southwest Harbor, Page 206

Top 12 Country Inns to Get Pampered
Saltair Inn, Bar Harbor, Page 232

7 Great Boutique Hotels
West Street Inn, Bar Harbor, Page 247

Have Tent, Will Travel, 10 Places to Camp
Blackwoods and Seawall Campgrounds, Acadia National Park, Page 252
Baxter State Park, Millinocket, Page 252

3 Favorite AMC Huts
Little Lyford, 100-Mile Wilderness, Page 256

Favorite Maine Huts & Trails Hut
Stratton Brook Hut, Page 258

Southern Maine

8 Summer Drives That Will Keep You Smiling
A Painterly Perspective, Kennebunkport to Cape Elizabeth, Page 15

Life's a Beach
Footbridge Beach, Ogunquit, Page 31
Popham Beach, Phippsburg, Page 31

10 Most Instagrammable Sites
Lobster Buoys on the Docks of Cape Porpoise, Page 32
The Boulder Strewn Coastline of Prouts Neck, Page
Portland Head Light, Portland, Page 32

3 Ways to Savor Lighthouses
Aboard the *J. & E. Riggin*, Sailing from Rockland, Page 33
On a Stroll Around Portland Head Light, Cape Elizabeth, Page 33

5 Quintessential New England Towns
Kennebunkport, Page 39

7 Best Bike Rides
Islesboro, Page 49

10 Classic New England Hikes
Maiden Cliff, Camden, Page 54

9 Exceptional Mountain Biking Locales
Bradbury Mountain State Park, Pownal, Page 68

Walk this Way, 17 Best Walks
The Marginal Way, Ogunquit, Page 78
Cliff Walk, Prouts Neck, Page 79
Rockland Breakwater, Rockland, Page 79

New England's Best Botanical Garden
Coastal Maine Botanical Garden, Boothbay Harbor, Page 80

4 Places to Sea Kayak
Peaks Island, Maine, Page 103
Sheepscot Bay, Georgetown, Page 103

6 Places to Sail
Penobscot Bay, Page 112

An Added Bonus! Aerial Adventures, Tubing, Sculling, and Stargazing
Viewing the Night Sky from Sandy Pines Campground, Kennebunkport, Page 121
Tubing the Ogunquit River, Ogunquit, Page 123

5 Retro Ski Resorts
Camden Snow Bowl, Camden, Page 125

11 Best Art Museums
Portland Museum of Art, Portland, Page 156
The Farnsworth, Rockland, Page 156

6 Hidden Art Historical Gems
The Olson House, Cushing, Page 158
Winslow Homer Studio, Prouts Neck, Page 159

7 Unique Places to See Regional Theatre/Dance/Films
Ogunquit Playhouse, Ogunquit, Page 175

5 Special Spots to See a Musical Performance
Stone Mountain Arts Center, Brownfield, Page 177

4 Authentic Guided Day Trips
Bike to 5 Lighthouses in Portland with Summer Feet
Cycling, Page 178

10 Best Family Experiences
Mr. Bean, Freeport, Page 186
Owl's Head Transportation Museum, Rockland,
Page 187

6 Favorite Lodgings for Family Get-Togethers
Sebasco Harbor Resort, Sebasco Estates, Page 197

5 Great Overnight Camps for Kids
Camp O-AT-K, Sebago, Page 201

6 Favorite Lobster/Clam Shacks
The Lobster Shack at Two Lights, Cape Elizabeth,
Page 205

McLoons Lobster, South Thomaston, Page 206

5 Unique Food Outings
The Maine Windjammer Lobster Bake, Penobscot Bay, Page 209

10 Best Places for Pizza
Otto Pizza, Portland, Page 217

3 Great Locales for Craft Beer Lovers
Portland, Page 221

Best Farm-Next-To-Table Dining Experience
Primo, Rockland, Page 222

Top 12 Country Inns to Get Pampered
Chebeague Island Inn, Chebeague Island, Page 231
Grey Havens Inn, Georgetown, Page 231

7 Best Resorts Along the Sea
Inn by the Sea, Crescent Beach, Page 236
Cliff House, Cape Neddick, Page 237
The Samoset, Rockport, Page 238

7 Great Boutique Hotels
Beachmere Inn, Ogunquit, Page 246
250 Main, Rockland, Page 246

Have Tent, Will Travel, 10 Places to Camp
Hermit Island Campground, Phippsburg, Page 251

Northern New Hampshire

3 Requisite Fall Foliage Drives
Kancamagus Highway, Page 13

8 Summer Drives That Will Keep You Smiling
Drive Through the Notches, Jackson to Dixville
Notch, Page 19

5 Quintessential New England Towns
Jackson, Page 38

10 Classic New England Hikes
Falling Waters/Old Bridle Path Loop, Franconia
Notch State Park, Page 51
Mount Willard, Crawford Notch, Page 52
Welch/Dickey Mountain Trail, Waterville Valley,
Page 53

9 Exceptional Mountain Biking Locales
Bartlett Experimental Forest, Bartlett, Page 67

Walk this Way, 17 Best Walks
Sabbaday Falls, Waterville Valley, Page 76

5 Great Fall Foliage Activities Away from the Crowds
Hike to Champney Falls off the Kancamagus
Highway, Page 94

5 Places to Canoe or Kayak
Umbagog Lake, Errol, Page 106
Saco River, Conway, Page 106

8 Places to Cross-Country Ski
Jackson Ski Touring Foundation, Jackson, Page 133
Bretton Woods Nordic Center, Bretton Woods, Page 133

Have Snowshoes, Will Travel
The 19-Mile Brook Trail to Carter Notch, Pinkham Notch, Page 135

6 Winter Adventures
Dogsled Umbagog Lake on the Maine/New Hampshire Border, Page 141
Hike and Ski at Tuckerman Ravine, Pinkham Notch, Page 142

10 Best Family Experiences
Story Land, Glen, Page 186

5 Great Overnight Camps for Kids
Camp Walt Whitman, Piermont, Page 201

10 Best Places for Pizza
Flatbread, North Conway, Page 217

4 Resorts in the Countryside
Omni Mount Washington Resort, Bretton Woods, Page 239

Have Tent, Will Travel, 10 Places to Camp
Lafayette Campground, Franconia Notch State Park, Page 251

3 Favorite AMC Huts
Lakes of the Clouds Hut, White Mountains, Page 255
Galehead Hut, White Mountains, Page 256

Southern New Hampshire

Life's a Beach
Odiorne Point State Park, Rye, Page 30

3 Ways to Savor Covered Bridges
Drive through 4 Covered Bridges, Swanzey, Page 36

10 Classic New England Hikes
Mount Monadnock, Jaffrey Center, Page 50

All Aboard, 6 Best Rail-to-Trails
Nashua River Rail Trail, Ayer, Massachusetts to Nashua, Page 65

9 Exceptional Mountain Biking Locales
Bear Brook State Park, Allenstown, Page 68

Walk this Way, 17 Best Walks
Fox Research and Demonstration Forest, Hillsborough, Page 76

5 Special Spots to Bird Watch
Odiorne Point State Park, Portsmouth, Page 99

8 Places to Cross-Country Ski
Windblown XC, New Ipswich, Page 132

6 Hidden Art Historical Gems
Baker Library, Dartmouth College, Hanover, Page 161

4 Authentic Guided Day Trips
Learn About the Ghosts and Goblins of Portsmouth, Page 180

10 Best Family Experiences
Strawbery Banke, Portsmouth, Page 185

6 Favorite Lodgings for Family Get-Togethers
The Inn at East Hill Farm, Troy Page 196

5 Great Overnight Camps for Kids
Camp Kebeyun, Alton Bay, Page 200

7 Great Boutique Hotels
Ale House Inn, Portsmouth, Page 245

Northern Vermont

3 Requisite Fall Foliage Drives
Route 100, Page 11

8 Summer Drives That Will Keep You Smiling
A Carpet of Velvety Green, St. Johnsbury to Lake Willoughby, Page 18

10 Most Instagrammable Sites
The Village Green at Craftsbury Common, Page 32

3 Ways to Savor Covered Bridges
Bike Through the Covered Bridges of Waitsfield and Warren, Page 35

5 Quintessential New England Towns
East Burke, Page 38

10 Classic New England Hikes
Mount Pisgah, West Burke, Page 57
Mount Mansfield, Stowe, Page 58

All Aboard, 6 Best Rail-to-Trails
Island Line, Burlington, Page 63

9 Exceptional Mountain Biking Locales
The Kingdom Trails, East Burke, Page 67
Millstone Hill Touring Center, Barre, Page 67

5 Great Fall Foliage Activities Away from the Crowds

Horseback Ride at Vermont Icelandic Horse Farm, Waitsfield, Page 95

6 Places to Sail

Burlington, Page 114

3 Best Swimming Holes

Boulder Beach State Park, Groton, Page 120

An Added Bonus! Aerial Adventures, Tubing, Sculling, and Stargazing

Sculling Hosmer Pond, Craftsbury, Page 123

5 Retro Ski Resorts

Mad River Glen, Waitsfield, Page 126

8 Places to Cross-Country Ski

Trapp Family Lodge, Stowe, Page 131
Darling Hill, East Burke, Page 132

Have Snowshoes, Will Travel

Smugglers' Notch, Route 108, Stowe, Page 134

6 Winter Adventures

Snowboarding the Backcountry, Stowe, Page 143

5 Best Spots to Relive History

Shelburne Museum, South Burlington, Page 150

6 Hidden Art Historical Gems
St. Johnsbury Athenaeum, St. Johnsbury, Page 159

5 Special Spots to See a Musical Performance
Trapp Family Lodge, Stowe, Page 177

4 Best Places to Apple/Strawberry Pick
Cold Hollow Cider Mill, Waterbury Center, Page 192

6 Favorite Lodgings for Family Get-Togethers
Tyler Place, Highland Springs, Page 196

5 Unique Food Outings
Ben & Jerry's Factory, Waterbury Center, Page 210

10 Best Places for Pizza
Pizza on Earth, Charlotte, Page 217

3 Great Locales for Craft Beer Lovers
Stowe, Page 219

Top 12 Country Inns to Get Pampered
The Pitcher Inn, Waitsfield, Page 230

Southern Vermont

8 Summer Drives That Will Keep You Smiling
Shoot the Gaps, Warren to Middlebury, Page 24

3 Ways to Savor Covered Bridges
Dine with View of a Covered Bridge, Quechee, Page 35

7 Best Bike Rides
Addison, Page 48

Walk this Way, 17 Best Walks
Marsh-Billings-Rockefeller National Historic Park, Woodstock, Page 77
West River Trail, Jamaica State Park, Page 77

5 Great Fall Foliage Activities Away from the Crowds
Golf the Equinox Course, Manchester, Page 95

5 Places to White Water Raft/Kayak
West River, Jamaica, Page 110

3 Places to Fish
Flyfishing the Mettawee and White Rivers, Page 117

5 Retro Ski Resorts
Middlebury College Snow Bowl, Ripton, Page 127
Suicide Six, Pomfret, Page 127

8 Places to Cross-Country Ski
Blueberry Hill, Goshen, Page 130
Grafton Ponds, Grafton, Page 131

6 Winter Adventures
Ice Fishing Harriman Reservoir, Wilmington, Page 143

6 Favorite Lodgings for Family Get-Togethers
Basin Harbor Club, Vergennes, Page 195

5 Great Overnight Camps for Kids
Camp Keewaydin and Songaweedin, Salisbury, Page 200

5 Unique Food Outings
A Visit to The Grafton Village Cheese Company, Grafton, Page 210

Top 12 Country Inns to Get Pampered
Grafton Inn, Grafton, Page 229

4 Resorts in the Countryside
Woodstock Inn, Woodstock, Page 240
Twin Farms, Barnard, Page 241
The Equinox Resort, Manchester Village, Page 241

Have Tent, Will Travel, 10 Places to Camp
Button Bay State Park, Addison, Page 251

Eastern Massachusetts

8 Summer Drives That Will Keep You Smiling
Cape Ann Cruise, Rockport to Ipswich, Page 21

Life's a Beach
Nauset Light Beach, Eastham, Page 28
South Beach, Martha's Vineyard, Page 29
Surfside Beach, Nantucket, Page 29
Crane Beach, Ipswich, Page 29
Wingaersheek Beach, Gloucester, Page 30

10 Most Instagrammable Sites
Gay Head Cliffs (Aquinnah) at Martha's Vineyard,
Page 32
Herring Cove Beach at Sunset, Provincetown, Page 32

3 Ways to Savor Lighthouses
The Perfect Place to Picnic, Great Point, Nantucket,
Page 34

7 Best Bike Rides
Westport, Page 46
Provincetown, Page 47
Nantucket, Page 47

All Aboard, 6 Best Rail-to-Trails
Cape Cod Rail Trail, Wellfleet to South Dennis,
Page 61

Minuteman Bikeway, Somerville, Page 64

Walk this Way, 17 Best Walks
World's End, Hingham, Page 73
Boston Harbor Islands, Boston, Page 73
Arnold Arboretum, Boston, Page 74
Fort Hill Trail, Eastham, Page 75
Broadmoor Wildlife Sanctuary, Natick, Page 75
Walden Pond, Concord, Page 76

8 Trustees of Reservations Sites Not To Be Overlooked
Long Hill, Beverly, Page 81
Westport Town Farm, Westport, Page 82
Mytoi and Cape Poge Wildlife Refuge, Martha's Vineyard, Page 82

5 Special Spots to Bird Watch
Plum Island, Newburyport, Page 98
Wellfleet Bay Wildlife Sanctuary, Wellfleet, Page 99

4 Places to Sea Kayak
Essex River Basin, Essex, Page 102

5 Places to Canoe or Kayak
Ipswich River, Topsfield, Page 107
Charles River, Boston, Page 107

6 Places to Sail
Boston Harbor Islands, Page 113
Buzzards Bay, Page 113

3 Places to Fish
Surfcasting for Stripers, Martha's Vineyard, Page 116
Cape Cod's Kettle Ponds, Page 117

3 Best Swimming Holes
Williams Pond, Wellfleet, Page 119

Have Snowshoes, Will Travel
Blue Hills Reservation, Milton, Page 136

5 Best Spots to Relive History
Freedom Trail, Boston, Page 147
Minute Man National Historic Park, Lexington and Concord, Page 148
New Bedford National Historic Park, New Bedford, Page 149

11 Best Art Museums
The Museum of Fine Arts, Boston, Page 151
The Harvard Art Museums, Cambridge, Page 152
Peabody Essex Museum, Salem, Page 152
Worcester Art Museum, Worcester, Page 153

4 Best Literary Landmarks
Orchard House, Concord, Page 167
House of Seven Gables, Salem, Page 167

Not Your Typical Walk in the Park, 3 Favorite Cemeteries
Mt. Auburn Cemetery, Watertown, Page 169
Forest Hills Cemetery, Jamaica Plain, Page 170
Granary Burying Ground, Boston, Page 170

5 Special Spots to See a Musical Performance

Shalin Liu Performance Center, Rockport, Page 176

Fenway Park, Boston, Page 176

4 Authentic Guided Day Trips

Drive the Dunes of Cape Cod with Art's Dune Tours, Page 179

10 Best Family Experiences

Museum of Science, Boston, Page 183

Salem Witch Museum, Salem, Page 184

Old Sturbridge Village, Sturbridge, Page 185

The Cape Cod League, Cape Cod, Page 185

5 Best Spots to See Wildlife

A Whale of a Good Time, Stellwagen Bank, Page 189

Finding Harbor Seals on Monomoy National Wildlife Refuge, Cape Cod, Page 189

4 Best Places to Apple/Strawberry Pick

Bolton Orchards, Bolton, Page 191

Russell Orchards, Ipswich, Page 191

6 Favorite Lodgings for Family Get-Togethers

The Winnetu, Martha's Vineyard, Page 193

Ocean Edge Resort, Brewster, Page 194

6 Favorite Lobster/Clam Shacks

Arnold's Lobster and Clam Bar, Eastham, Page 206

Woodman's, Essex, Page 207

The Clam Box, Ipswich, Page 208

5 Unique Food Outings
Portuguese Fare in New Bedford, Page 211
Massachusetts Historic Hole-in-the-Wall Joints, Page 211

10 Best Places for Pizza
Santarpio's, East Boston, Page 216
Enrico's Pizza, Fiskdale, Page 216

3 Great Locales for Craft Beer Lovers
Metrowest Boston, Page 220

Top 12 Country Inns to Get Pampered
The Inn at Castle Hill, Ipswich, Page 226
Blue, Plum Island, Page 227
Salt House Inn, Provincetown, Page 228
Union Street Inn, Nantucket, Page 228

7 Best Resorts Along the Sea
Wequassett Resort, Harwich, Page 234
Chatham Bars Inn, Chatham, Page 235
The Wauwinet, Nantucket, Page 235

Have Tent, Will Travel, 10 Places to Camp
Nickerson State Park, Brewster, Page 250
Boston Harbor Islands, Boston, Page 73

Western Massachusetts

3 Requisite Fall Foliage Drives
The Mohawk Trail,

10 Most Instagrammable Sites
Bash Bish Falls, Mount Washington,

10 Classic New England Hike
Monument Mountain, Great Barrington,

All Aboard, 6 Best Rail-to-Trails
Norwottuck Rail Trail, Northampton,

9 Exceptional Mountain Biking Locales
Savoy Mountain State Forest, Florida,

8 Trustees of Reservations Sites Not To Be Overlooked
Tully Lake Campground, Royalston,
Chesterfield Gorge, Chesterfield,
William Cullen Bryant Homestead, Cummington,
Naumkeag, Stockbridge,
Bartholomew's Cobble, Sheffield,

5 Places to White Water Raft/Kayak
Deerfield River, Charlemont,

3 Best Swimming Holes
Bash Bish Falls, Mt. Washington, Page 119

An Added Bonus! Aerial Adventures, Tubing, Sculling, and Stargazing
Catamount Aerial Adventure Park, South Egremont, Page 122

5 Retro Ski Resorts
Butternut Basin, Great Barrington, Page 128

8 Places to Cross-Country Ski
Notchview, Dalton, Page 129

Have Snowshoes, Will Travel
October Mountain State Forest, Lee, Page 136

11 Best Art Museums
Norman Rockwell Museum, Stockbridge, Page 154
Clark Art Institute, Williamstown, Page 155
Mass MoCA, North Adams, Page 155

7 Unique Places to See Regional Theatre/Dance/Films
Williamstown Theatre Festival, Williamstown, Page 173
Colonial Theatre, Pittsfield, Page 173
Jacob's Pillow, Becket, Page 174
Academy of Music Theatre, Northampton, Page 174

5 Special Spots to See a Musical Performance
Tanglewood, Lenox, Page 176

10 Best Family Experiences
Eric Carle Museum, Amherst, Page 184

5 Great Overnight Camps for Kids
Camp Schodack (Nassau, New York, just across the Mass line), Page 199

5 Unique Food Outings
Massachusetts Historic Hole-in-the-Wall Joints, Page 211

Top 12 Country Inns to Get Pampered
The Guest House at Field Farm, Williamstown, Page 229

Have Tent, Will Travel, 10 Places to Camp,
Mount Greylock State Reservation, Adams, Page 249

Rhode Island

8 Summer Drives That Will Keep You Smiling
Rhode Island Beach Ramble, Wickford to Watch Hill, Page 20

Life's a Beach
East Beach, Charlestown, Page 27
Second Beach, Middletown, Page 27

10 Most Instagrammable Sites
The Cliff Walk Behind the Mansions of Newport, Page 32

5 Quintessential New England Towns
Little Compton, Page 40

7 Best Bike Rides
Block Island, Page 43
Little Compton, Page 45

All Aboard, 6 Best Rail-to-Trails
East Bay Bicycle Path, Providence to Bristol, Page 62

9 Exceptional Mountain Biking Locales
Arcadia Management Area, Hope Valley, Page 69

Walk this Way, 17 Best Walks
Napatree Point, Westerly, Page 72

Cliff Walk, Newport, Page 72

6 Places to Sail
Newport, Page 111

5 Best Spots to Relive History
The Mansions, Newport, Page 150

7 Unique Places to See Regional Theatre/Dance/ Films
Trinity Rep, Providence, Page 175

4 Authentic Guided Day Trips
Race a Genuine America's Cup 12-meter Yacht in Newport, Page 179

10 Best Places for Pizza
Caserta Pizzeria, Providence, Page 215
Al Forno, Providence Page 215

Top 12 Country Inns to Get Pampered
Cliffside Inn, Newport, Page 226

7 Best Resorts Along the Sea
Ocean House, Watch Hill, Page 233

7 Great Boutique Hotels
Weekapaug Inn, Weekapaug, Page 244

Have Tent, Will Travel, 10 Places to Camp
Charlestown Breachway, Page 249

Eastern Connecticut

8 Summer Drives That Will Keep You Smiling
Connecticut River Amble, Old Saybrook to Hadlyme,
Page 17

Life's a Beach
Hammonasset Beach, Madison, Page 26

5 Quintessential New England Towns
Madison, Page 39

9 Exceptional Mountain Biking Locales
Pachaug State Forest, Voluntown, Page 70
Bluff Point Beach, Groton, Page 70

Walk this Way, 17 Best Walks
Harkness Memorial State Park, Waterford, Page 71

4 Places to Sea Kayak
Thimble Islands, Branford, Page 102

11 Best Art Museums
Wadsworth Athenaeum, Hartford, Page 154
Yale Center for British Art, New Haven, Page 154

6 Hidden Art Historical Gems
New London Post Office, New London, Page 163

4 Best Literary Landmarks
Mark Twain House, Hartford, Page 166
Harriet Beecher Stowe House, Hartford, Page 166

7 Unique Places to See Regional Theatre/Dance/Films
Goodspeed Opera House, East Haddam, Page 175

10 Best Family Experiences
Mystic Seaport, Mystic, Page 184

5 Best Spots to See Wildlife
Penguin Encounter, Mystic Aquarium, Mystic, Page 190

4 Best Places to Apple/Strawberry Pick
B. F. Clyde's, Mystic, Page 192

10 Best Places for Pizza
Frank Pepe Pizzeria Napoletana, New Haven, Page 213
Sally's Apizza, New Haven, Page 214
Modern Apizza, New Haven, Page 214

7 Great Boutique Hotels
Spicer Mansion, Mystic, Page 244

Have Tent, Will Travel, 10 Places to Camp
Lake Waramaug State Park, New Preston, Page 248

Western Connecticut

Life's a Beach
Compo Beach, Westport, Page 26

Walk this Way, 17 Best Walks
Earthplace, the Nature Discovery Center, Westport, Page 71

5 Special Spots to Bird Watch
Connecticut Audubon Coastal Center, Milford Point, Page 98

Have Snowshoes, Will Travel
Ten Mile Hill, Kent, Page 137

6 Hidden Art Historical Gems
Weir Farm National Historic Site, Wilton, Page 164

A Stop to Antique Shop
Woodbury, Page 172

Top 12 Country Inns to Get Pampered
The Mayflower Inn, Washington, Page 225

7 Great Boutique Hotels
Winvian Farm, Morris, Page 243

CPSIA information can be obtained
at www.ICGtesting.com
Printed in the USA
BVHW061135230620
582158BV00012B/541